GOLDENTREE BIBLIOGRAPHIES

O. B. Hardison, Jr.

Editor

Linguistics
and
English Linguistics

compiled by

Harold B. Allen

University of Minnesota

APPLETON-CENTURY-CROFTS

Educational Division

New York   MEREDITH   CORPORATION

Preface

THE FOLLOWING BIBLIOGRAPHY is intended for graduate and advanced undergraduate students who desire a convenient guide to linguistic scholarship in English, education, linguistics, and related areas. The listing is necessarily selective, but every effort has been made to provide ample coverage of the major fields and topics, with emphasis on works published in the twentieth century.

In order to keep this bibliography to a practical size a great number of pertinent references had to be left out. With a bare handful of exceptions in two or three categories, the classes of excluded references are as follows:

Materials in a language other than English

Books or articles published prior to 1922, except for a few seminal works (see entry 1.17)

Freshman textbooks and anthologies

Popular and semi-popular books and articles on language

Articles each of which is devoted to the discussion of a single word

Articles on current British English as a whole, without expressed relevance to American English

Articles in collections already listed, unless an anthologized article is particularly significant or likely to be overlooked because its content is not suggested by the title of the collection

Doctoral dissertations abstracted in *Microfilm Abstracts* or *Dissertation Abstracts,* but not otherwise available in printed form

In general, the compiler has attempted to steer a middle course between the brief lists of references in the average textbook and the long professional bibliography in which significant items are often lost in the sheer number of references given. This bibliography should materially assist the student in his effort to survey a topic, write reports and term papers, prepare for examinations, and do independent reading. Attention is called to four features intended to enhance its utility.

(1) Extra margin on each page permits listing of library call-numbers of often used items.

(2) Extra space at the bottom of each page permits inclusion of additional entries; blank pages for notes follow the final page of entries.

(3) An index by author follows the bibliography proper.

(4) The index and cross-reference numbers direct the reader to the page and position-on-the-page of the desired entry. Thus, in an entry such as

EDMUNDSON, H. P., ed. "A statistician's view of linguistic models and language-data processing," *Natural Language and the Computer* [**10**.11], 151-79.

the number **10**.11 indicates that the entry referred to is on page 10, and is the 11th item on that page. Both page numbers and individual entry numbers are conspicuous in size and position so that the process of finding entries is fast as well as simple.

Journals whose abbreviations are not listed in the PMLA bibliography are as follows:

AA   American Anthropologist

CAn   Current Anthropologist

CCC   (NCTE)   College Composition and Communication (National Council of Teachers of English)

FL   Foundations of Language (Dordrecht, Holland)

JASP   Journal of Abnormal and Social Psychology

JL   Journal of Linguistics (Cambridge, England)

P( )ICL   Proceedings of the First (Second, Third, etc.) International Congress of Linguists (see **6**.15)

P( )ICPS   Proceedings of the First (Second, etc.) International Congress of Phonetic Sciences (see **6**.16)

SML   Statistical Methods in Linguistics (Stockholm)

An asterisk following an entry indicates a work of "special importance" in the field. Other annotations, given in brackets, which may conclude an entry are: (1) abbreviations of paperback publishers and series numbers, all based on the list of abbreviations given in *Paperbound Books in Print;* (2) cross reference(s) to other entries in the bibliography in which the work cited is also included; (3) a phrase describing the subject of an allusive title.

Note: *The publisher and editor invite suggestions for additions to future printings of the bibliography.*

Contents

1

Bibliographies

Some specialized bibliographies are listed in appropriate sections.

1 *American Speech*. New York: Columbia University Press, 1925– . Bibliographies: "Present-day English," quarterly; "General and historical studies," May and Dec. issues; "Phonetics," Feb. and Oct. issues.*

2 *Annual Bibliography of English Language and Literature, 1920–* . (In progress.) Cambridge: Cambridge University Press, 1921– .

3 *Bibliography of the Summer Institute of Linguistics*. Santa Ana, Calif.: Summer Institute of Linguistics, 1964.

4 Booth, T. Y. "The cliché: a working bibliography," *BB* 33:61-3 (1960).

5 Boyd, Julian C., and Harold V. King. "Annotated bibliography of generative grammar," *LL* 12:4.307-12 (1962).

6 Bursill-Hall, G. L. "Bibliography: Theories of syntactic analysis," *SIL* 16.100-12 (1962).

7 Comité International Permanent des Linguistes. *Bibliographie linguistique de l'année 19–* et complément des années précédentes. Utrecht and Antwerp, 1949 and annually thereafter. Vols. I and II cover the years 1939–1947.*

8 Delavenay, Émile, and K. Delavenay. *Bibliography of Mechanical Translation*. 's-Gravenhage: Mouton, 1960.

9 *Dissertations in Linguistics: 1957–63*. Washington: Center for Applied Linguistics, 1964.

10 Frank, Marcella. *Annotated Bibliography of Materials for English as a Second Language*. New York: National Ass'n for Foreign Student Affairs, 1960 [Pamphlet].

11 Gage, William W. *Contrastive Studies in Linguistics: A Bibliographical Checklist*. Washington: Center for Applied Linguistics, 1961.

12 Goodell, R. J. "An ethnolinguistic bibliography with supporting material in linguistics and anthropology," *AnL* 6:2.10-32 (1964).

13 Hamp, Eric P. "Selected summary bibliography of language classifications," *SIL* 15.29-45 (1960).

14 Haugen, Einar. "Bilingualism in the Americas: A bibliography and research guide," *PADS* 26 (1956).*

15 Hayes, Francis. "Gestures: a working bibliography," *SFQ* 21.218-317 (1957).

16 Juilland, Alphonse G. "A bibliography of diachronic phonemics," *Word* 9.198-208 (1953).

17 Kennedy, Arthur G. *A Bibliography of Writings on the English Language*, from the beginning of printing to the end of 1922 (1927). New York: Hafner, 1961.

18 Kurath, Hans. "A bibliography of American pronunciation 1888–1928," *Lang* 5.155-62 (1929).

19 Leopold, Werner F. *Bibliography of Child Language*. (*NUSH* No. 28). Evanston, Ill.: Northwestern Univ. Press, 1952.*

20 "Linguistica Canadiana," *CJL* 9:2.117-24 (1964). [A linguistic bibliography for 1963 and supplement for previous years.]

21 *Modern Language Journal*. Annual annotated bibliography of modern language methodology. 1916– .*

1 MORGAN, Bayard Quincy. "A critical bibliography of works on translation." *On Translation*[88.15], pp. 271-93.

2 NOSTRAND, Howard Lee, *et al. Research on Language Teaching: An Annotated International Bibliography for 1945–61.* Seattle: University of Washington Press, 1962; 2nd edition, 1965.*

3 OHANNESSIAN, Sirarpi, ed. *Reference List of Materials for English as a Second Language.* Washington: Center for Applied Linguistics, 1964.*

4 PIETRZYK, Alfred, *et al.,* eds. *Selected Titles in Sociolinguistics.* Washington: Center for Applied Linguistics, 1964.

5 *Publication of the Modern Language Association of America.* Annual bibliography, 1956–   Menasha, Wis.: Modern Language Assoc.*

6 RICE, Frank, and Allene GUSS, eds. *Information Sources in Linguistics.* Washington: Center for Applied Linguistics, 1965.*

7 SCHEURWEGHS, Gustav, ed. *Analytical Bibliography of Writings on Modern English Morphology and Syntax, 1877–1960.* With an appendix on Japanese publications by Hideo Yamaguchi. Part 1, Periodical literature and miscellanies of the United States and Western and Northern Europe; Part 2, Studies in bookform. Louvain: University of Louvain, 1963, 1964.

8 SEBEOK, Thomas A. "Selected readings in general phonemics (1925–1964)," *SIL* 17.3-9 (1964).

9 SEELY, Pauline A., and Richard B. SEALOCK. *A Bibliography of Place Name Literature, United States and Canada.* Chicago: American Library Assoc., 1948. Supplements in *Names* 3.102-16 (1955); 6.26-50 (1958); 7.203-32 (1959); 9.165-74 (1961); 11.115-27 (1963).*

10 SMITH, Elsdon C. "Literature of personal names in English, 1953," *Names* 2.144-7 (1954, and annually thereafter).*

Dictionaries and Glossaries

Some specialized dictionaries are listed in the appropriate sections.

11 *Acronyms Dictionary.* Detroit: Gale Research Co., 1961.

12 ADAMS, Raymond F. *Western Words: A Dictionary of the Range, Cow Camp and Trail.* Norman: University of Oklahoma Press, 1944.

13 AITKEN, A. J., ed. *A Dictionary of the Older Scottish Tongue: From the Twelfth Century to the End of the Seventeenth.* (In 25 parts.) Pts. 1-20. Chicago: University of Chicago Press, 1933-64. (In progress.) *

14 BAKER, Sidney John. *A Popular Dictionary of Australian Slang,* 3d edition. Melbourne: Robertson & Mullens, 1943.

15 BARNHART, Clarence L., and W. D. HALSEY, eds. *The New Century Encyclopedia of Names.* 3 vols. New York: Appleton-Century-Crofts, 1954.

16 BENSE, J. F. *A Dictionary of the Low-Dutch Element in the English Vocabulary.* 's-Gravenhage: Martinus Nijhoff, 1939.

17 BUCK, Carl D., *et al. A Dictionary of Selected Synonyms in the Principal Indo-European Languages; A Contribution to the History of Ideas.* Chicago: University of Chicago Press, 1949.*

18 CRAIGIE, Sir William, J. R. HULBERT, *et al.,* eds. *A Dictionary of American English on Historical Principles.* 4 vols. Chicago: Univ. of Chicago Press, 1936.*

DICTIONARIES & GLOSSARIES

3

1 EKWALL, Eilert. *The Concise Oxford Dictionary of English Place-names,* 4th ed. Oxford: Oxford Univ. Press, 1960.

2 EVANS, Bergen, and Cornelia EVANS. *A Dictionary of American Usage.* New York: Random House, 1957.

3 FEILITZEN, Olof von. *The Pre-Conquest Personal Names of Domesday Book.* (Nomina Germanica, Arkiv för Germansk Namnforskning, No. 3). Uppsala: Almqvist & Wiksell, 1937.

4 FOWLER, H. W. *A Dictionary of Modern English Usage.* Oxford: Clarendon Press, 1959. [British usage.]

5 FRANKLYN, Julian. *A Dictionary of Nicknames.* London: H. Hamilton, 1962. New York: British Book Centre.

6 FRANKLYN, Julian. *A Dictionary of Rhyming Slang.* New York: Hillary House, 1961.

7 FREEMAN, William. *A Concise Dictionary of English Idioms.* New York: Crowell, 1951.

8 GRANT, William, and David MURISON, eds. *The Scottish National Dictionary.* Edinburgh: Scottish National Dictionary Assoc. [Publication in fascicles began in 1931 and reached the letter N in 1964.] *

9 GREET, W. Cabell. *World Words; Recommended Pronunciations.* New York: Columbia Univ. Press, 1948.

10 GROSE, Francis. *A Classical Dictionary of the Vulgar Tongue,* third edition (1796). Edited with a biographical and critical sketch and commentary by Eric Partridge. London: Routledge and Kegan Paul, 1963.

11 HALL, John R. C. *A Concise Anglo-Saxon Dictionary,* 4th ed., with supp. by Herbert D. Merritt. Cambridge: Cambridge Univ. Press, 1961.

12 HAMP, Eric P. *A Glossary of American Technical Linguistic Usage,* 2nd edition. Utrecht and Antwerp: Spectrum, 1963.

13 HORWILL, H. W. *A Dictionary of Modern American Usage.* Oxford: Oxford University Press, 1935.

14 HUNT, Cecil. *A Dictionary of Word Makers: Pen Pictures of the People behind Our Language.* New York: Philosophical Library, 1949. See also "Biographies of Linguists," p. **19.**

15 JONES, Daniel. *Everyman's English Pronouncing Dictionary; Containing 58,000 Words in International Phonetic Transcription,* 11th edition. London: Dent, 1956. [Glossary and Bibliography; an American edition. New York: Dutton, 1956.] *

16 KENYON, John S., and Thomas A. KNOTT, eds. *A Pronouncing Dictionary of American English.* Springfield, Mass.: G. & C. Merriam, 1953.*

17 KURATH, Hans, and Sherman M. KUHN, eds. *Middle English Dictionary.* Ann Arbor: Univ. of Michigan Press, 1954– . (In progress; A-H now published.) *

18 LOUGHEAD, Flora H. *Dictionary of Given Names, with the Origins and Meanings.* Glendale, Calif.: A. H. Clark, 1934.

19 MAINE, G. F., ed. *The New Modern Etymological Dictionary,* rev. edition. London: Collins, 1957.

20 MATHEWS, Mitford M., ed. *A Dictionary of Americanisms on Historical Principles,* 2 vols. Chicago: Univ. of Chicago Press, 1951; one vol. edition, 1956.*

21 MERITT, Herbert Dean. *Old English Glosses* (a Collection). New York: Mod. Lang. Assn., 1945.

1   *Oxford English Dictionary.* A corrected re-issue of *A New English Dictionary on Historical Principles,* with an introduction, supplement, and bibliography. Oxford: Clarendon Press, 1933.*

2   PARTRIDGE, Eric, ed. *Dictionary of Clichés,* 4th edition. New York: Macmillan, 1950.

3   PARTRIDGE, Eric, ed. *A Dictionary of Slang and Unconventional English,* 5th edition. New York: Macmillan, 1961.*

4   PARTRIDGE, Eric, ed. *A Dictionary of the Underworld, British and American.* Reprinted with new addenda. London: Routledge and Kegan Paul, 1961.

5   PARTRIDGE, Eric. *Origins, a Short Etymological Dictionary of the English Language.* London: Routledge and Kegan Paul, 1958.

6   PEI, M. A., and Frank GAYNOR, eds. *A Dictionary of Linguistics.* New York: Philosophical Library, 1954.

7   REANEY, P. H. A., ed. *A Dictionary of British Surnames.* London: Routledge and Kegan Paul, 1958.

8   RUFFNER, Frederick G., and Robert C. THOMAS, eds. *Code Names Dictionary* (Introduction by Eric Partridge). Detroit: Gale Research, 1963.

9   SCOTT, G. R. *Swan's Anglo-American Dictionary.* New York: Library Publishers, 1952.

10   SKEAT, Walter W. *Etymological Dictionary of the English Language,* 4th edition. Oxford: Clarendon Press, 1910.*

11   TOLLER, T. N. *An Anglo-Saxon Dictionary Based on the Manuscript Collections of the Late Joseph Bosworth.* Oxford: Oxford Univ. Press, 1882-98; with *Supplements,* 1908-20.*

12   TRENCH, R. C., ed. *Dictionary of Obsolete English.* London: Hulton Press, 1959.

13   TURNER, R. Lister. *A Comparative Dictionary of Indo-Aryan Languages.* New York: Oxford Univ. Press, 1962– . (In progress.)

14   WEEKLEY, Ernest. *A Concise Etymological Dictionary of Modern English,* rev. edition. London: Secker and Warberg, 1952.

15   WEINGARTEN, Joseph A. *An American Dictionary of Slang and Colloquial English.* Brooklyn, New York: Weingarten, 1955.

16   WENTWORTH, Harold, ed. *American Dialect Dictionary.* New York: Crowell, 1944.

17   WENTWORTH, Harold, and Stuart Berg FLEXNER, eds. *Dictionary of American Slang.* New York: Crowell, 1960.*

18   WITHYCOMBE, E. J. *The Oxford Dictionary of English Christian Names.* Oxford: Clarendon, 1945.

19   WRIGHT, Joseph, ed. *The English Dialect Dictionary.* 6 vols. New York: Hacker Art Books, 1963.*

5

Festschriften and Miscellaneous Collections

Anthologies in specialized fields are usually listed in the appropriate sections.

1   ALLEN, Harold B., ed. *Readings in Applied English Linguistics,* 2nd edition. New York: Appleton-Century-Crofts, 1964. [Cited herein as RAEL.]

2   BLACK, Max, ed. *The Importance of Language.* Englewood Cliffs, N.J.: Prentice-Hall, 1962. [Spec S-37.]

3   BEHRE, Frank, ed. *Contributions to English Syntax and Philology.* GothSE, 14. Gothenburg: Almqvist and Wiksell, 1962.

4   BEHRE, Frank. *Papers on English Vocabulary and Syntax,* Alvar Ellegård and Yngve Olsson, eds. GothSE, 10. Gothenburg: Almqvist and Wiksell, 1961.

5   BRADLEY, Henry. *The Collected Papers of Henry Bradley.* (With a memoir by Robert Bridges.) Oxford: Clarendon Press, 1928.

6   CAFFEE, Nathaniel M., and Thomas A. KIRBY, eds. *Studies for William A. Read.* University, La.: Louisiana State Univ. Press, 1940.

7   Communications Research Centre, Univ. of London, eds. *Aspects of Translation.* London: Secker and Warburg, 1958; Philadelphia: Dufour Editions, 1959.

8   Communications Research Centre, Univ. of London, eds. *Studies in Communication.* London: Secker and Warburg, 1955.

9   DAVIS, Norman, and C. L. WRENN, eds. *English and Medieval Studies Presented to J. R. R. Tolkien on the Occasion of His Seventieth Birthday.* London: Allen and Unwin, 1962.

10   FODOR, Jerry A., and Jerrold J. KATZ, eds. *The Structure of Language, Readings in the Philosophy of Language.* Englewood Cliffs, N.J.: Prentice-Hall, 1964. [Cited herein as *Structure of Language: Readings.*]

11   FRY, Dennis B., *et al.,* eds. *In Honour of Daniel Jones.* London: Longmans, Green, 1964.

12   Georgetown University, School of Foreign Service. *Reports of the Round Table Meetings on Linguistics and Language Teachings.* Washington: Georgetown Univ. Press, 1951– .

13   GRAVIT, Francis W., and Albert VALDMAN, eds. *Structural Drill and the Language Laboratory.* Report of the Third Language Laboratory Conference held at Indiana University, March, 1962. *PRCAFL,* 27. Bloomington, Ind.: Indiana Univ. and 's-Gravenhage: Mouton, 1963. [Issued also as Part III of *IJAL* 29:2.]

14   GREENBERG, Joseph H., ed. *Universals of Language.* Cambridge, Mass.: M.I.T. Press, 1963.

15   GUMPERZ, John J., and Dell HYMES, eds. *The Ethnography of Communication.* Menasha, Wis.: American Anthropological Association, 1964. (Issued as *AA* 66, No. 6, Pt. 2. Special Publication.)

16   HALLE, Morris, ed. *For Roman Jakobson.* 's-Gravenhage: Mouton, 1956.

17   HATFIELD, James T., *et al.,* eds. *Curme Volume of Linguistic Studies.* Language Monograph No. 7, Linguistic Society of America, 1930.

18   HAYAKAWA, S. I., ed. *Language, Meaning and Maturity* (Review of General Semantics, 1943–53). *Our Language and Our World* (Review of General Semantics, 1953–58). New York: Harper and Row, 1954 and 1959.

6 COLLECTIONS

1 HAYAKAWA, S. I., ed. *The Use and Misuse of Language.* Selected essays from *ETC.* Greenwich, Conn.: Fawcett Publs., 1962. [Prem T166.]

2 HENLE, Paul, ed. *Language, Thought, and Culture.* Ann Arbor: Univ. of Michigan Press, 1958.

3 HYMES, Dell, ed. *Language in Culture and Society.* New York: Harper and Row, 1965.

4 JAKOBSON, Roman. *Selected Writings. Vol. I: Phonological Studies.* 's-Gravenhage: Mouton, 1960.

5 JAKOBSON, Roman, ed. *Structure of Language and Its Mathematical Aspects.* Proceedings of Symposia in Applied Mathematics, Vol. 12 (1960). Providence, R.I.: American Mathematical Society, 1961. [Cited herein as *Structure of Language.*]

6 Joos, Martin, ed. *Readings in Linguistics: The Development of Descriptive Linguistics in America since 1925.* 4th edition. Washington: American Council of Learned Societies, 1966.

7 KAISER, Louise, ed. *Manual of Phonetics.* New York: Humanities Press, 1957.

8 KIRBY, Thomas A., and Henry Bosley WOOLF, eds. *Philologica: the Malone Anniversary Studies.* Baltimore: The Johns Hopkins Press, 1949.

9 KROEBER, A. L., *et al.*, eds. *Anthropology Today: An Encyclopedic Inventory.* Chicago: Univ. of Chicago Press, 1953.

10 MALONE, Kemp, and Martin B. RUUD, eds. *Studies in English Philology: A Miscellany in Honor of Frederick Klaeber.* Minneapolis: Univ. of Minnesota Press, 1929. [Cited herein as *Klaeber Miscellany.*]

11 MARCKWARDT, Albert H., ed. *Studies in Languages and Linguistics in Honor of Charles C. Fries.* Ann Arbor: The English Language Institute, The Univ. of Michigan, 1964.

12 *Mélanges de Linguistique et de Philologie: Fernand Mossé in Memoriam.* (Centre National de la Recherche Scientifique.) Paris: Didier, 1959.

13 *Philological Miscellany Presented to Eilert Ekwall.* Uppsala: Lundequist, 1942.

14 *Philological Society,* London, eds. *Studies in Linguistic Analysis.* Oxford: Blackwell, 1957.

15 *Proceedings of the International Congress of Linguists,* 1930– . Various titles and places of publication. In this bibliography articles are cited from the *Proceedings of the Seventh Congress,* London, 1956 [*P7ICL*], *The Eighth Congress,* Oslo, 1958 [*P8ICL*], and *The Ninth Congress,* 's-Gravenhage, 1964 [*P9ICL*].

16 *Proceedings of the International Congress of Phonetic Sciences.* Places of publication vary. Cited in this bibliography are the *Second International Congress,* London, 1936 [*P2ICPS*], and the *Fourth International Congress,* 's-Gravenhage, 1963 [*P4ICPS*].

17 PULGRAM, Ernst, ed. *Studies Presented to Joshua Whatmough on his Sixtieth Birthday.* 's-Gravenhage: Mouton, 1957.

18 SAPIR, Edward. *Selected Writings of Edward Sapir,* David G. Mandelbaum, ed. Berkeley & Los Angeles: Univ. of California Press, 1950.

19 SAPORTA, Sol, ed. *Psycholinguistics.* New York: Holt, Rinehart and Winston, 1961.

20 SEBEOK, Thomas A., ed. *Style in Language.* Cambridge: M.I.T. Press; New York: Wiley, 1960.

21 SHENTON, Herbert N., Edward SAPIR, and Otto JESPERSEN. *International Communications: A Symposium on the Language Problem.* London: Kegan Paul, Trench, Trubner, 1931.

1 SPIER, Leslie, *et al. Language, Culture, and Personality*. Essays in Memory of E. Sapir. Menasha, Wis.: Banta, 1941.

2 TAX, Sol, Loren C. EISELEY, Irving ROUSE, and Carl VOEGELIN, eds. *An Appraisal of Anthropology Today*. Chicago: Chicago Univ. Press, 1963.

3 UNESCO. *Scientific and Technical Translating, and Other Aspects of the Language Problem*, 2nd edition. Paris: UNESCO, 1958.

Linguistics

General Linguistics

4 ALLEN, William Stannard. *On the Linguistic Study of Languages; An Inaugural Lecture*. London: Cambridge Univ. Press, 1957.

5 BLOOMFIELD, Leonard. *Language*. New York: Holt, Rinehart and Winston, 1933.*

6 BOLLING, George Melville. "Linguistics and philology," *Lang* 5.27-32 (1929).

7 CANNON, Carland. "Linguistics as a science." *QJS* 51.68-82 (1965).

8 CLEATOR, P. E. *Lost Languages*. New York: John Day, 1959. [Mentor MT427.]

9 DE LAGUNA, Grace A. *Speech: Its Function and Development*. New Haven: Yale Univ. Press, 1927.

10 ENTWISTLE, William J. *Aspects of Language*. London: Faber and Faber, 1953.

11 FIRTH, John R. *Papers in Linguistics, 1934–1951*. London: Oxford Univ. Press, 1957.

12 FIRTH, John R. *The Tongues of Men*. London: Watts, 1937.

13 GARDINER, Sir Alan. *The Theory of Speech and Language,* 2nd edition. Oxford: Clarendon, 1951.

14 GLEASON, H. A., Jr. *An Introduction to Descriptive Linguistics,* 2nd edition. New York: Holt, Rinehart and Winston, 1961. [With workbook.] *

15 GRAFF, Willem L. *Language and Languages: An Introduction to Linguistics*. New York: Appleton-Century-Crofts, 1932.

16 GRAY, Louis H. *Foundations of Language*. New York: Macmillan, 1939.

17 GREENBERG, Joseph H. *Essays in Linguistics*. Chicago: Univ. of Chicago Press, 1957. [Phoen P119.]

18 HALL, Robert A., Jr. *Introductory Linguistics*. Philadelphia: Chilton, 1964.

19 HALL, Robert A., Jr. *Linguistics and Your Language*. New York: Doubleday, 1960. [Anch A201.]

20 HERDAN, Gustav. *Language as Choice and Change*. Groningen: Noordhoff, 1956.

21 HILL, Archibald A. *Introduction to Linguistic Structures: From Sound to Sentence in English*. New York: Harcourt, Brace and World, 1958.*

22 HJELMSLEV, Louis. *Prolegomena to a Theory of Language*. Tr. by Francis J. Whitfield, rev. Eng. ed. Madison: Univ. of Wisconsin Press, 1961.*

23 HOCKETT, Charles F. *A Course in Modern Linguistics*. New York: Macmillan, 1958.

8   LINGUISTICS

1   HUGHES, John P. *The Science of Language.* New York: Random House, 1962.

2   JAKOBSON, Roman, and Morris HALLE. *Fundamentals of Language.* 's-Gravenhage: Mouton, 1956.

3   JESPERSEN, Otto. *Language: Its Nature, Development, and Origin.* London: Allen and Unwin, 1922. [Nort N229.] *

4   JESPERSEN, Otto. *Linguistica.* Copenhagen: Munksgaard, 1933.

5   JESPERSEN, Otto. *The Philosophy of Grammar.* London: Allen and Unwin, 1924.*

6   LEHMANN, Winfred P. *Historical Linguistics: An Introduction.* New York: Holt, Rinehart and Winston, 1962. [With workbook.]

7   MALMBERG, Bertil. *Structural Linguistics and Human Communication.* Berlin: Springer, 1963; New York: Academic Press, 1963.

8   MARTINET, André. *A Functional View of Language.* Oxford: Clarendon Press, 1962.*

9   ORNSTEIN, Jacob, and William W. GAGE. *The ABC's of Languages and Linguistics.* Philadelphia: Chilton Books, 1964.

10   PAUL, Hermann. *Principles of the History of Language.* Tr. by H. A. Strong. New York: Macmillan, 1889.*

11   POTTER, Simeon. *Language in the Modern World.* London: Penguin Books, 1960.

12   POTTER, Simeon. *Modern Linguistics.* London: André Deutsch, 1957. [Nort N223.]

13   ROBINS, R. H. *General Linguistics: An Introductory Survey.* London: Longmans, Green, 1964; Bloomington: Indiana Univ. Press, 1964.

14   SAPIR, Edward. *Language: An Introduction to the Study of Speech.* Harcourt, Brace and World, 1921.* [Harvest HB7.]

15   SAUSSURE, Ferdinand de. *A Course in General Linguistics.* Transl. by Wade Baskin. New York: Philosophical Library, 1959. [16524-McGH] *

16   SCHLAUCH, Margaret. *The Gift of Language.* New York: Dover Publications, 1955. [Reissue of *The Gift of Tongues.* New York: Modern Age Books, 1942.]

17   STURTEVANT, Edgar H. *An Introduction to Linguistic Science.* New Haven: Yale Univ. Press, (1947) 1960. [Yale Y-17.]

18   STURTEVANT, Edgar H. *Linguistic Change: an Introduction to the Historical Study of Language.* Reprint edition. New York: G. E. Stechert, 1942. [Phoen P60.]

19   VENDRYES, J. *Language: A Linguistic Introduction to History.* Tr. by Paul Radin (1925). New York: Barnes and Noble, 1951.

20   VOEGELIN, Carl F. and Florence M., eds. "Languages of the world," a publication of the Archives of the Languages of the World. *AnL* 6 (Sino-Tibetan Fascicle One), no. 3; (Indo-Pacific Fascicle One), no. 4; (African Fascicle One), no. 5; (Native American Fascicle One), no. 6; (Indo-Pacific Fascicle Two), no. 7; (Ibero-Caucasian and Pidgin Creole Fascicle One), no. 8; (Indo-Pacific Fascicle Three), no. 9 (1964); vol. 7 (Boreo-Oriental Fascicle One), no. 1 (1965).

21   WATERMAN, John T. *Perspectives in Linguistics.* Chicago: Univ. of Chicago Press, 1963. [Phoen P106.]

22   WHATMOUGH, Joshua. *Language: A Modern Synthesis.* New York: St. Martin's Press, 1956. [Ment—MD209.]

1 WHITNEY, William Dwight. *Language and the Study of Language,* 10th edition. New York: Scribner's 1910.

2 WHITNEY, William Dwight. *The Life and Growth of Language: An Outline of Linguistic Science.* New York: Appleton-Century-Crofts, 1875.

3 WILSON, N. L. *The Concept of Language.* Toronto: Univ. of Toronto Press, 1958.

Communication Theory and Information Theory

4 AYER, A. J., *et al. Studies in Communication.* London: London Univ., 1955.*

5 BERRY, J. "Some statistical aspects of conversational speech," *Communication Theory* [9.11], 392-401.

6 BRILLOUIN, Leon B. *Science and Information Theory,* second edition. New York: Academic Press, 1962.

7 CHERRY, E. Colin. *On Human Communication: A Review, a Survey, and a Criticism.* Cambridge: M.I.T. Press; and New York: Wiley, 1957.

8 CHERRY, E. Colin. "Roman Jakobson's 'distinctive features' as normal coordinates of language," *For Roman Jakobson* [5.16], 60-64.

9 HARRAH, David. *Communication: A Logical Model.* Cambridge: M.I.T. Press, 1963.

10 HEFFERLINE, Ralph F. "Communication theory: I. Integrator of the arts all sciences; II. Extension to intrapersonal behavior," *QJS* 41.223-33; 365-76 (1955).

11 JACKSON, W., ed. *Communication Theory.* London: Butterworth Scientific Publications, 1953.

12 JAKOBSON, Roman. "Linguistics and communication theory," *Structure of Language* [6.5], 245-52.

13 KARLGREN, Hans. "Information measures," *P9ICL* [6.15] 804-12.

14 McMILLAN, Brockway, ed. *Current Trends in Information Theory.* Pittsburgh: Univ. of Pittsburgh, 1953.

15 MILLER, George A. *Language and Communication.* New York: McGraw-Hill, 1963 (corrected re-issue of 1951 edition). [McGH 42001.]

16 SHANNON, Claude E., and Warren WEAVER. *The Mathematical Theory of Communication.* Urbana: Univ. of Illinois Press, 1959. [Illini IB13.]*

17 WELLS, Rulon. "A measure of subjective information," *Structure of Language.* [6.5], 237-44.

Computational and Mathematical Linguistics, Machine Translation, and Information Retrieval

See also 1.8 and 1.21.

18 AKHMANOVA, O. S., *et al. Exact Methods in Linguistic Research.* Berkeley: Univ. of California Press, 1963.

19 BAR-HILLEL, Yehoshua. "Idioms," *Machine Translation of Languages* [11.6], 183-93.

20 BOOTH, Andrew D., L. BRANDWOOD, and J. P. CHASE. *Mechanical Resolution of Linguistic Problems.* New York: Academic Press, 1958.*

21 CLEAVE, John P. "A model for mechanical translation," *MT* 4.2-4 (1957); "A type of program for mechanical translation," *MT* 4.54-8 (1957).

1 CROSSLAND, R. A. "Graphic linguistics and its terminology," *MT* 3.8-13 (1956).

2 DELAVENAY, Émile. *An Introduction to Machine Translation.* London: Thames & Hudson, 1960.

3 EDMUNDSON, H. P., ed. *Proceedings of the National Symposium on Machine Translation.* Englewood Cliffs; N. J.: Prentice-Hall, 1961.

4 EDMUNDSON, H. P. "A statistician's view of linguistic models and language-data processing," *Natural Language and the Computer* [**10**.11], 151-79.

5 ELLEGÅRD, Alvar. "Notes on the use of statistical methods in the studies of name vocabularies," *SN* 30.214-31 (1958).

6 ELLEGÅRD, Alvar. "Statistical measurement of linguistic relationship," *Lang* 35.131-56 (1959).

7 GARVIN, Paul L. "Computer participation in linguistic research," *Lang* 38.385-89 (1962).

8 GARVIN, Paul L. "The impact of language data processing upon linguistic analysis," *P9ICL* [**6**.15], 706-12 (1964).

9 GARVIN, Paul L. "A linguist's view of language-data processing," *Natural Language and the Computer* [**10**.11], 107-27.

10 GARVIN, Paul L. "Machine translation," *P8ICL* [**6**.15], 502-10.

11 GARVIN, Paul L., ed. *Natural Language and the Computer.* New York: McGraw-Hill, 1963.*

12 GARVIN, Paul L. "Some linguistic problems in machine translation," *For Roman Jakobson* [**5**.16], 180-6.

13 GARVIN, Paul L. "Syntax in machine translation," *Natural Language and the Computer* [**10**.11], 223-32.

14 GARVIN, Paul L., and Edith Crowell TRAGER. "The conversion of phonetic into orthographic English: a machine-translation approach to the problem," *Phonetica* 11.1-18 (1964).

15 GARVIN, Paul L., and W. KARUSH. "Linguistics, data processing, and mathematics," *Natural Language and the Computer* [**10**.11], 357-69.

16 HALLIDAY, M. A. K. "Linguistics and machine translation," *ZPSK* 15.145-58 (1962).

17 HARPER, Kenneth E. "Dictionary problems in machine translation," *Natural Language and the Computer* [**10**.11], 215-22.

18 HAYS, David G. *Bibliography of Computational Linguistics.* Santa Monica, Calif.: Rand Corporation, 1965.

19 HAYS, David G. "Research procedures in machine translation," *Natural Language and the Computer* [**10**.11], 183-214.

20 HERDAN, Gustav. *Type-token Mathematics: A Textbook of Mathematical Linguistics.* 's-Gravenhage: Mouton, 1960.*

21 HUMECKY, Assya, and Andreas KOUTSOUDAS. "Some further results on the resolution of ambiguity of syntactic function by linear context," *L&S* 4.146-49 (1961).

22 IVANOV, Vyacheslav. "Cybernetics and the science of language," *MLJ* 46.158-59 (1962).

23 JOYNES, Mary Lu, and Winfred P. LEHMANN. "Linguistic theories underlying the work of various MT groups," *Linguistics* 8.62-71 (1964).

24 KELLOGG, Dimitri A. *Machine Translation: A Review and Analysis Report.* Washington: U. S. Government Printing Office, 1961.

LINGUISTICS

11

1 KOUTSOUDAS, Andreas, and R. KORFHAGE. "Mechanical translation and the problem of multiple meaning," *MT* 3.46-51,61 (1956).

2 KUČERA, Henry. "A note on the digital computer in linguistics," *Lang* 38.279-82 (1962).

3 LAMB, Sydney M. "The digital computer as an aid in linguistics," *Lang* 37.382-414 (1961).

4 LEVIN, Samuel R. "On automatic production of poetic sequences," *TSLL* 5.138-46 (1963).

5 LOCKE, William N. "Speech typewriters and translating machines," *PMLA* 70.23-32 (1955).

6 LOCKE, William N., and A. Donald BOOTH, eds. *Machine Translation of Languages: Fourteen Essays.* Cambridge: M.I.T. Press; and New York: Wiley, 1955. [Bib.]

7 MARON, M. E. "A logician's view of language-data processing," *Natural Language and the Computer* [**10**.11], 128-50.

8 MELKANOFF, Michel A. "Computer languages," *Natural Language and the Computer* [**10**.11], 84-94.

9 MERSEL, Jules. "Programming aspects in machine translation," *Natural Language and the Computer* [**10**.11], 233-51.

10 OETTINGER, Anthony G. *Automatic Language Translation: Lexical and Technical Aspects, with Particular Reference to Russian.* [Introd. by Joshua Whatmough.] (Harvard Monographs in Applied Science, No. 8.) Cambridge: Harvard Univ. Press, 1960.

11 PARKER-RHODES, A. F. "The use of statistics in language research," *MT* 5.67-72 (1958).

12 PLATH, Warren. "Mathematical linguistics," *Trends* [**18**.25], 21-57.

13 RAY, L. C. "Programming for natural language," *Natural Language and the Computer* [**10**.11], 95-105.

14 REIFLER, Erwin. "The mechanical determination of meaning," *Machine Translation of Languages* [**11**.6], 136-64.

15 SEBEOK, Thomas A. "The informational model of language: analog and digital coding in animal and human communication," *Natural Language and the Computer* [**10**.11], 47-64.

16 SWANSON, Don R. "The formulation of the retrieval problem," *Natural Language and the Computer* [**10**.11], 255-67.

17 TRAVIS, Larry E. "Analytic information retrieval," *Natural Language and the Computer* [**10**.11], 310-53.

18 WEAVER, Warren. "Translation," *Machine Translation of Languages* [**11**.6], 15-23.

19 WHATMOUGH, Joshua. "Mathematical linguistics," *P8ICL* [**6**.15], 62-73.

20 WOODBURY, David O. "The translating machine," *Atlantic,* Aug., 1959, 60-64.

21 YNGVE, Victor H. "Syntax and the problem of multiple meaning," *Machine Translation of Languages* [**11**.6], 208-26.

Linguistic Theory

See also 1.6, **72**.14, and **83**.3.

22 ALKON, Paul K. "Behaviourism and linguistics; an historical note," *L&S* 2.37-51 (1959).

12

1 ANDREYEV, N. D. "Models as a tool in the development of linguistic theory," *Word* 18.186-97 (1962).

2 ANDRE[Y]EV, N. D., and L. R. ZINDER. "On the notions of the speech act, speech, speech probability, and language," *Linguistics* 4.5-13 (1964).

3 AVRAM, Andrei. "Some thoughts on the functional yield of phonemic oppositions," *Linguistics* 5.40-47 (1964).

4 BAR-HILLEL, Yehoshua. "Logical syntax and semantics," *Lang* 30.230-37 (1954).

5 BAZELL, C. E. "The choice of criteria in structural linguistics," *Word* 10.126-35 (1954).

6 BAZELL, C. E. *Linguistic Form.* Istanbul: Istanbul Press, 1953.*

7 BAZELL, C. E. "On form and function," *JEGP* 37.329-31 (1939).

8 BAZELL, C. E. "Phonemic and morphemic analysis," *Word* 8.33-8 (1952).

9 BLOCH, Bernard, and George L. TRAGER. *Outline of Linguistic Analysis.* Baltimore: Linguistic Society of America, 1942.*

10 BLOOMFIELD, Leonard. *Linguistic Aspects of Science.* Chicago: Univ. of Chicago Press, 1939.*

11 BLOOMFIELD, Leonard. *Outline Guide for the Practical Study of Foreign Languages.* Baltimore: Ling. Soc. of America, 1942.*

12 BLOOMFIELD, Leonard. "A set of postulates for the science of language," *Lang* 2.153-64 (1926).*

13 BOLINGER, Dwight L. "Linguistic science and linguistic engineering," *Word* 16.374-91 (1960). See **15**.21.

14 BOLINGER, Dwight L. "A theory of pitch accent in English," *Word* 14.109-49 (1958).

15 BONFANTE, Giuliano. "The neolinguistic position," *Lang* 23.344-75 (1947).

16 BONFANTE, Giuliano. "On reconstruction and linguistic method," Part 1, *Word* 1.83-94 (1945); Part 2, *Word* 1.132-61 (1945); "Additional notes on reconstruction," *Word* 2.155-6 (1946).

17 BRITTON, Karl. *Communication: A Philosophical Study of Language.* London: Kegan Paul, Trench, & Trubner, 1939; New York: Harcourt, Brace and World, 1939.

18 BULL, William E. *Time, Tense, and the Verb: A Study in Theoretical and Applied Linguistics, with Particular Attention to Spanish.* UCPL, Vol. 19. Berkeley: Univ. of Calif. Press, 1960.

19 BURKE, Kenneth. "A dramatistic view of the origins of language," *QJS* 38.251-64, 446-460 (1952); 39.79-92 (1953); "Postscripts on the negative," *QJS* 39.209-16 (1953).

20 CHARNLEY, M. Bertens. "The eventuative relation," *SN* 26.99-103 (1954).

21 CHATMAN, Seymour. "Immediate constituents and expansion analysis," *Word* 11.377-85 (1955).

22 CHOMSKY, Noam. *Current Issues in Linguistic Theory.* (Janua Linguarum, series minor, no. 38) 's-Gravenhage: Mouton, 1964.

23 CHOMSKY, Noam. "The logical basis of linguistic theory," *P9ICL* [**6**.15], 914-75. With bibl. and discussion, 975-1007. Revised and expanded in *Structure of Language: Readings* [**6**.5], 50-114. With bibl.*

24 COLLINGE, N. E. "Some linguistic paradoxes," *JL* 1.1-12 (1965). [Inconsistencies in linguistic theory.]

1 CONTRERAS, Heles, and Sol SAPORTA. "The validation of a phonological grammar." *Lingua* 9.1-15 (1960).

2 DeGROOT, A. Willem. "Classification of cases and uses of cases." *For Roman Jakobson* [5.16], 187-94.

3 DIEBOLD, A. Richard, Jr. "Determining the centers of dispersal of language groups," *IJAL* 26.1-10 (1960).

4 DRIVER, Harold Edson. "An integration of functional, evolutionary, and historical theory by means of correlations," Memoir XII, *IJAL,* Supp. to 22:1. 1-35 (1956).

5 DYEN, Isidore. "Language distribution and migration theory," *Lang* 32.611-26 (1956).

6 EMENEAU, Murray B. "Language and non-linguistic patterns," *Lang* 26.199-209 (1950).

7 FISHMAN, Joshua A. "Language maintenance and language shift as a field of inquiry," *Linguistics* 9.32-70 (1964). [Bib.]

8 FUNKE, Otto. "On the system of grammar," *ArL* 6.1-19 (1954).

9 GAMMON, Edward R. "On representing syntactic structure," *Lang* 39.369-97 (1963).

10 GARVIN, Paul L. "The definitional model of language," *Natural Language and the Computer* [**10**.11], 3-22.

11 HAAS, William. "Linguistic structures," *Word* 16:2 251-76 (1960).

12 HAAS, William. "On defining linguistic units," *TPS* 54-84 (1954).

13 HAAS, William. "Zero in linguistic description." *Studies in Linguistic Analysis* [**6**.14], 33-53.

14 HALLE, Morris. On the role of simplicity in linguistic descriptions," *Structure of Language* [**6**.5], 89-94.

15 HALLIDAY, M. A. K. "Categories of the theory of grammar," *Word* 17.241-92 (1961).

16 HARRIS, Zellig S. "Discontinuous morphemes." *Lang* 21.121-7 (1945).*

17 HARRIS, Zellig S. "Distributional structure," *Word* 10.146-62 (1954).

18 HARRIS, Zellig S. "From morpheme to utterance," *Lang* 22.161-83 (1946).*

19 HARRIS, Zellig S. *Methods in Structural Linguistics.* Chicago: Univ. of Chicago Press, 1951. [Phoen P-52.]

20 HARRIS, Zellig S. *String Analysis of Sentence Structure.* 's-Gravenhage: Mouton, 1962.*

21 HAUGEN, Einar. "The syllable in linguistic description," *For Roman Jakobson* [5.16], 213-21.

22 HILL, Archibald A., ed. *First Texas Conference on Problems of Linguistic Analysis in English, 1956.* Austin: Univ. of Texas, 1962.

23 HILL, Archibald A. "A postulate for linguistics in the sixties," *Lang* 38.345-51 (1962).

24 HILL, Archibald A., ed. *Second Texas Conference on Problems of Linguistic Analysis in English, 1957.* Austin: Univ. of Texas, 1962.

25 HILL, Archibald A., ed. *Third Texas Conference on Problems of Linguistic Analysis in English, 1958.* Austin: Univ. of Texas, 1962.

26 HOCKETT, Charles F. "Grammar for the hearer," *Structure of Language* [**6**.5], 220-36.

14 LINGUISTICS

1 Hockett, Charles F. "Implications of Bloomfield's Algonquian studies," *Lang* 24.117-31 (1948). Also in *Readings in Linguistics* [6.6], 280-89.

2 Hockett, Charles F. "Linguistic elements and their relations," *Lang* 37.29-53 (1961).

3 Hockett, Charles F. "Two models of grammatical description," *Word* 10.210-34 (1954).*

4 Hoenigswald, Henry M. "Sound change and linguistic structure," *Lang* 22.138-43 (1946). Also in *Readings in Linguistics* [6.6], 139-41.

5 Householder, Fred W. "On linguistic primes," *Word* 15.231-9 (1959).

6 Householder, Fred W., "On some recent claims in phonological theory," *JL* 1.13-34 (1965).

7 Hymes, Dell. "Positional analysis of categories," *Word* 11.10-23 (1955).

8 Joos, Martin. "Description of language design," *JAS* 22.701-8 (1950). Also in *Readings in Linguistics* [6.6], 349-56.

9 Juilland, Alphonse G. *Structural Relations.* 's-Gravenhage: Mouton, 1961.

10 Katz, Jerrold J. "Mentalism in linguistics," *Lang* 40.124-37 (1964).

11 Katz, Jerrold J., and Paul M. Postal. *An Integrated Theory of Linguistic Descriptions.* Cambridge, Mass.: M.I.T. Press, 1964.*

12 Kurath, Hans. "The binary interpretation of English vowels," *Lang* 33.111-22 (1957).

13 Leopold, Werner F. "Polarity in language," *Curme Studies* [5.17], 102-9.

14 Long, Ralph B. "The case for word grammar," *Third Texas Conference* [13.25], 34-55.

15 Martinet, André. "Diffusion of language and structural linguistics," *RPh* 6.5-13 (1953).

16 Martinet, André. "Elements of a functional syntax," *Word* 16:1.1-10 (1960).

17 Murra, John V., Robert M. Hankin, and Fred Holling. *The Soviet Linguistic Controversy,* New York: King's Crown Press, 1951.

18 Nida, Eugene A. "Linguistic and semantic structure," *Fries Studies* [6.11], 13-33.

19 Pike, Kenneth L. "Beyond the sentence," *CCC* (NCTE) 15.129-35 (1964).

20 Pike, Kenneth L. "Dimensions of grammatical constructions." *Lang* 38.221-44 (1962).

21 Pike, Kenneth L. "Grammemic theory." *GL* 2.35-41 (1957).*

22 Pike, Kenneth L. "Interpenetration of phonology, morphology, and syntax." *P8ICL* [6.15], 363-71.

23 Pike, Kenneth L. "Language as particle, wave, and field," *TQ* 2.37-54 (1959).

24 Pike, Kenneth L. "Nucleation." *MLJ* 44.291-5 (1960). Also in *TESL* [71.1].

25 Pike, Kenneth L. "A syntactic paradigm." *Lang* 39.216-30 (1963).

26 Pittman, Richard S. "Nuclear structures in linguistics," *Lang* 24.287-92 (1948).*

27 Pittman, Richard S. "On defining morphology and syntax," *IJAL* 25.199-201 (1959).

15

1 PULGRAM, Ernst. "Family tree, wave theory and dialectology," *Orbis* 2.67-72 (1953).

2 READ, Allen Walker. "The splitting and coalescence of widespread languages," *P9ICL* [6.15], 1129-34.

3 ROBINS, R. H. "Grammar, meaning, and the study of language," *CJL* 9:2.98-114 (1964).

4 ROBINS, R. H. "Some considerations on the status of grammar in linguistics," *ArL* 11.91-114 (1959).

5 SMITH, Henry Lee, Jr. "Syntactic analysis and a general theory of levels," *Third Texas Conference* [13.25], 86-107.

6 SPRINGER, George W. *Early Soviet Theories in Communication*. Cambridge, Mass.: Center for Intern'l Studies, M.I.T., 1956.

7 TRAGER, George L. "The systematization of the Whorf hypothesis," *AnL* 1:1.31-6 (1959).

8 TWADDELL, W. Freeman. "Uses and abuses of symmetry," *Second Texas Conference* [13.24], 129-37. [With discussion.]

9 ULDALL, H. J. *Outline of Glossematics: a Study in the Methodology of the Humanities with Special Reference to Linguistics. Part I, General Theory*. Copenhagen: Nordisk Sprog -og Kulturforlag, 1957.*

10 VOEGELIN, Carl F. "Model-directed structuralization," *AnL* 1.9-26 (1959).

11 WATERHOUSE, Viola. "Independent and dependent sentences," *IJAL* 29.45-54 (1963).

12 WELLS, R. S. "Immediate constituents," *Lang* 23.81-117 (1947).*

13 WHORF, Benjamin Lee. *Language, Thought, and Reality*. John B. Carroll, ed. Cambridge: M.I.T. Press; and New York: Wiley, 1957. [MIT 5.] *

14 ZIFF, Paul. "About what an adequate grammar couldn't do," *FL* 1.5-13 (1965).

Generative Grammar and Transformation Grammar

See also **1**.5, **70**.9, **87**.6, and **87**.16.

15 BACH, Emmon. *An Introduction to Transformational Grammars*. New York: Holt, Rinehart and Winston, 1964.

16 BACH, Emmon. "Some notes on the constituent structure of noun phrases," *AS* 38.295-7 (1963).

17 BACH, Emmon. "Subcategories in transformational grammars," *P9ICL* [6.15], 672-78.

18 BELASCO, Simon. "Tagmemics and transformational grammar in linguistic analysis," *Linguistics* 10.5-15 (1964).

19 CARROLL, John B. "An operational model for language behavior," *AnL* 1:1.37-54 (1959).*

20 CHOMSKY, Noam. "On the notion 'Rule of grammar,'" *Structure of Language* [6.5], 6-24.

21 CHOMSKY, Noam. "Some methodological remarks on generative grammar," *Word* 17.219-39 (1961). Repr. in *RAEL* [5.1], 173-91, and *Structure of Language: Readings* [5.10], 384-99. A reply to Archibald A. Hill, "Grammaticality," *Word* 17.1-10 (1961), also in *RAEL* [5.1], 163-72.

22 CHOMSKY, Noam. *Syntactic Structures*. 's-Gravenhage: Mouton, 1957; 4th printing, 1964.*

1 CHOMSKY, Noam. "A transformational approach to syntax," *Third Texas Conference* [13.25], 124-58. Repr. in *Structure of Language: Readings* [5.10], 211-45.

2 CHOMSKY, Noam, and George A. MILLER. "Introduction to the formal analysis of natural languages," *Handbook of Mathematical Psychology,* vol. 2, R. Duncan Luce, et al., eds. New York: Wiley, 1963, 269-321.

3 FILLMORE, Charles J. "The position of embedding transformations in a grammar," *Word* 19.208-31 (1963).

4 HALLE, Morris. "Phonology in generative grammar," *Word* 18.54-72 (1962).

5 HARMAN, Gilbert H. "Generative grammars without transformation rules; a defense of phrase structure," *Lang* 39.597-616 (1963).

6 HARRIS, Zellig S. "Co-occurrence and transformation in linguistic structure," *Lang* 33.283-340 (1957).*

7 HARRIS, Zellig S. "Discourse analysis," *Lang.* 28.1-30 (1952).*

8 HARRIS, Zellig S. "The transformational model of language structure," *AnL* 1.1.27-30 (1959).

9 KATZ, Jerrold J. "Semi-sentences," *Structure of Language: Readings* [5.10], 400-16.

10 KLIMA, Edward S. "Negation in English," *Structure of Language: Readings* [5.10], 246-323.

11 LEES, Robert B. "The constituent structure of noun phrases," *AS* 36.159-68 (1961).

12 LEES, Robert B. *The Grammar of English Nominalizations.* Bloomington: Research Center in Anthropology, Folklore, and Linguistics, Publication No. 12 (Indiana Univ., 1960, rev. 1963).*

13 LEES, Robert B. "Grammatical analysis of the English comparative construction," *Word* 17.171-85 (1961).

14 LEES, Robert B. "A multiply ambiguous adjectival construction in English," *Lang* 36.207-21 (1960).

15 LEES, Robert B. Review of Noam Chomsky, *Syntactic Structures* (1957), *Lang* 33.375-408 (1957).*

16 LEES, Robert B. "Transformation grammars and the Fries framework," *RAEL* [5.1], 137-46.

17 LEES, Robert B., and E. S. KLIMA. "Rules for English pronominalization," *Lang* 39.17-28 (1963).

18 LONGACRE, Robert E. "String constituent analysis," *Lang* 36.63-88 (1960).

19 MACLAY, Howard, and Mary D. SLEATOR. "Responses to language: judgments of grammaticalness," *IJAL* 26.275-82 (1960). See **15**.21.

20 MATTHEWS, P. H. "Problems of selection in transformation grammar," *JL* 1.35-47 (1965).

21 MATTHEWS, P. H. "Transformational grammar," *ArL* 13.196-209 (1961).

22 NORMAN, Arthur M. Z. "An outline of the subclasses of the English nominal," *AS* 33.83-9 (1958). Also in *RAEL* [5.1], 156-63.

23 POSTAL, Paul M. "Underlying and superficial linguistic structure," *HER* 34.246-66 (Spring, 1964).

24 PUTNAM, Hilary. "Some issues in the theory of grammar," *Structure of Language* [6.5], 25-42. [With special reference to Chomsky.]

1 ROBERTS, Paul. *English Syntax,* alternate edition. New York: Harcourt, Brace and World, 1964.

2 SCHACHTER, Paul. "Kernel and non-kernel sentences in transformational grammar," *P9ICL* [**6.**15], 692-96.

3 SMITH, Carlota S. "A class of complex modifiers in English," *Lang* 37.342-65 (1961).

4 SMITH, Carlota S. "Determiners and relative clauses in a generative grammar of English," *Lang* 40.37-52 (1964).

5 STOCKWELL, Robert P. "The place of intonation in a generative grammar of English," *Lang* 36.360-67 (1960). Also in *RAEL* [**5.**1], 192-200.

6 STOCKWELL, Robert P. "Transformational grammar in perspective," *English Studies Today,* third series, 51-66. Edinburgh: University Press, 1964.

7 STOCKWELL, Robert P. "The transformational model of generative or predictive grammar," *Natural Language and the Computer* [**10.**11], 23-46.

8 UHLENBECK, E. M. "An appraisal of transformation theory," *Lingua* 12.1-18 (1963).

9 VIERTEL, John. "Generative grammars," *CCC* (NCTE) 15.65-81 (1964).

10 VOEGELIN, C. F. "The generative criterion for deciding alternatives in descriptive linguistics," *SIL* 16.42-8 (1962).

11 YNGVE, Victor H. "A model and an hypothesis for language structure," *Proceedings of the American Philosophical Society* 104.444-466 (1960).*

Study of Linguistics and of Grammar, and the History of Linguistic Thought

12 ABERCROMBIE, David. "Forgotten phoneticians," *TPS* 1-34 (1948).

13 ALLEN, D. C. "Some theories of the growth and origin of language in Milton's age," *PQ* 28.5-16, 329 (1949).

14 BROUGH, John. "Theories of general linguistics in the Sanskrit grammarians," *TPS* (Oxford), 1951, 27-46.

15 BURSILL-HALL, G. L. "Levels analysis: J. R. Firth's theories of linguistic analysis," *JCLA* 6.124-35 (1960); 6.164-91 (1961).

16 BURSILL-HALL, G. L. "Medieval grammatical theories," *CJL* 9.40-54 (1963).

17 CARROLL, John B. *The Study of Language,* a survey of linguistics and related disciplines in America. Cambridge: Harvard University Press, 1953.*

18 DANIELSSON, Bror. *John Hart's Works on English Orthography and Pronunciation* (1551, 1569, 1570), Pt. I. Stockholm: Almqvist and Wiksell, 1955.

19 DANIELSSON, Bror. "A note on Edmund Coote. Prolegomena for a critical edition of Coote's 'English School-Master' (1596)," *SN* 32.228-40 (1960); "A second note on Edmund Coote," *SN* 33.282-84 (1961).

20 DYKEMA, Karl W. "Where our grammar came from," *College English* 22.455-465 (1961).

21 EDGERTON, Franklin. "Notes on early American work in linguistics," *PAPS* 87.25-34 (1943).

22 EDGERTON, Franklin. "Panini, Sanskrit grammarian," *WSt* 27.3-5 (1952).

1 FIRTH, John R. "The English school of phonetics." *TPS, 1946,* 92-132 (1947).

2 FIRTH, John R. "A synopsis of linguistic theory. 1930-1955." *Studies in Linguistic Analysis* [6.14], 1-32.

3 FOWKES, Robert A. "Friedrich Hebbel and comparative linguistics." *GR* 30.294-300 (1955).

4 FRIES, Charles C. "The Bloomfield 'School'." *Trends* [18.25], 196-224.

5 FUNKE, Otto. "Ben Jonson's *English Grammar* (1640)." *Anglia* 64.117-34 (1940).

6 FUNKE, Otto. "On the sources of John Wilkins' Philosophical Language (1668)." *ES* 40.208-14 (1959).

7 GIVNER, David A. "Scientific preconceptions in Locke's Philosophy of Language." *JHI* 23.340-54 (1962).

8 HALL, Robert A., Jr. "American linguistics, 1925-50," *Archivum Linguisticum* 3.101-125 (1951) and 4.1-16 (1952).

9 HALL, Robert A., Jr. "Benedetto Croce and 'Idealistic Linguistics'," *SIL* 6.27-35 (1947).

10 HALL, Robert A., Jr. "Linguistic theory in the Italian Renaissance," *Lang* 12.96-107 (1936).

11 HARRIS, Zellig S. "Program of the Prague phonologists," *AS* 11.107-15 (1936).

12 HARTUNG, Charles V. "The scope of linguistic study." *QJS* 50.1-12 (1964).

13 HAUGEN, Einar. "Directions in modern linguistics." *Lang* 27.211-22 (1951). Repr. in *Readings in Linguistics* [6.6], 357-63.

14 HOENIGSWALD, Henry M. "On the history of the comparative method." *AnL* 5:1.1-11 (1963).

15 JAKOBSON, Roman. "Franz Boas' approach to language." *IJAL* 10.185-95 (1944). See also 15.21.

16 JONES, Daniel. *The History and Meaning of the Term* Phoneme. *MPhon,* Suppl. to No. 108 (1957).

17 KRÁMSKÝ, Jiří. "Quantitative phonemics in the last decade," *Phonetica* 8.166-85 (1963).

18 LANDRUM, Grace W. "The first colonial grammars in English." *William and Mary Coll. Qtly.* 19.272-85 (1939).

19 LANE, George S. "Change of emphasis in linguistics with particular reference to Paul and Bloomfield." *SP* 42.465-83 (1945).

20 LANE, George S. "On the present state of Indo-European linguistics." *Lang* 25.333-42 (1949).

21 LEOPOLD, Werner F. "Roman Jakobson and the study of child language." *For Roman Jakobson* [5.16], 285-8.

22 MATTHEWS, W. K. "Phonetics and phonology in retrospect." *Lingua* 7.254-68 (1958).

23 MATTHEWS, William. "William Tiffin, 18th century phonetician." *ES* 18.97-114 (1936).

24 MEECH, Sanford B. "An early treatise in English concerning Latin grammar," *Essays and Studies by Members of the Eng. Dept. of the Univ. of Michigan,* 1935, 81-125.

25 MOHRMANN, Christine, Alf SOMMERFELT, and Joshua WHATMOUGH, eds. *Trends in European and American Linguistics,* 1930-1960. Utrecht, Spectrum, 1961. Cited as *Trends.**

1 Moses, Elbert R., Jr. *Phonetics: History and Interpretation.* New York: Prentice-Hall, 1964. [Bib.] *

2 Pedersen, Holger. *Linguistic Science in the Nineteenth Century,* trans. John Webster Spargo. Cambridge: Harvard Univ. Press, 1931; repr. as *The Discovery of Language.* Bloomington: Indiana Univ. Press, 1962. [Ind. MB-40.] *

3 Pyles, Thomas. "The role of historical linguistics," *CE* 26.292-8 (1965).

4 Read, Allen Walker. "The motivation of Lindley Murray's grammatical work," *JEGP* 38.525-39 (1939).

5 Robins, R. H. *Ancient and Medieval Grammatical Theory in Europe.* London: G. Bell and Sons, Ltd., 1951.

6 Salmon, Vivian. "Thomas Hayward, grammarian," *Neophil* 43.64-74 (1959).

7 Scheurweghs, Gustave, and E. Vorlat. "Problems of the history of English grammar," *Eng. Studien* 40.135-43 (1959).

8 Sugg, Redding S., Jr. "The mood of eighteenth-century English grammar," *PQ* 43.239-52 (1964).

9 Trager, George L. "Changes of emphasis in linguistics," *SP* 43.461-4 (1946).

10 Vallins, G. H. "Cobbett's 'Grammar'," *English* (London) 10.48-53 (1954).

11 Voegelin, Carl F. and Florence M. "On the history of structuralizing in 20th century America," *AnL* 5:1.12-37 (1963).

12 Voegelin, Carl F., and Zellig S. Harris. "The scope of linguistics," *AA* 49.588-600 (1947).

13 Vorlat, E. "The sources of Lindley Murray's 'The English Grammar'," *LB* 48.108-25 (1959).

14 Wells, Rulon S. "De Saussure's system of linguistics," *Word* 3.1-31 (1947). Also in *Readings in Linguistics* [6.6], 1-18.

Biographies of Linguists

See also **3.14.**

15 Bloch, Bernard. "Leonard Bloomfield," *Lang* 25.87-94 (bib., 94-98) (1949).

16 Carnochan, J. "J. R. Firth," *MPhon* 115.2-3 (1961).

17 Emeneau, Murray B. "Franklin Edgerton," *Lang* 40.111-23 (1964).

18 Hackett, Herbert. "Bronislaw Malinowski," *WSt* 32:2.1-4 (1956).

19 Hahn, E. Adelaide. "Edgar Howard Sturtevant," *Lang* 28.417-34 (1952).

20 Hatfield, James T. "George Oliver Curme, a biographical sketch," *Curme Studies* [5.17].

21 Hoenigswald, Henry M. "George Melville Bolling," *Lang* 40.329-36 (1964). [Bib.]

22 Hymes, Dell. "Alfred Louis Kroeber," *Lang* 37.1-28 (1961).

23 Lane, George S. "Carl Darling Buck," *Lang* 31.181-9 (1955).

24 McDavid, Raven I., Jr. "Hans Kurath," *Orbis* 9.597-610 (1960).

25 Warfel, Harry R. *Noah Webster, Schoolmaster to America.* New York: Macmillan, 1936.

26 Waterman, John T. "Ferdinand de Saussure—forerunner of modern structuralism," *MLJ* 40.307-9 (1956).

20 LINGUISTICS

1 WRENN, C. L. "Henry Sweet," *TPS* (1946) 177-201 (1947).

2 ZANDVOORT, R. W. "Three grammarians: Poutsma—Jespersen—Kruisinga," *MSpr* 52.2-14 (1958).

Morphemics

See also "MORPHEMICS," p. 50.

3 BAZELL, C. E. "On the problem of the morpheme," *ArL* 1.1-15 (1949).

4 BOLINGER, Dwight L. "On defining the morpheme," *Word* 4.18-23 (1948).

5 FOWLER, Roger. " 'Meaning' and the theory of the morpheme," *Lingua* 12.165-76 (1963).

6 GARVIN, Paul L. "On the relative tractability of morphological data," *Word* 13.12-23 (1957).

7 HARRIS, Zellig S. "From phoneme to morpheme," *Lang* 31.190-222 (1955).

8 HOCKETT, Charles F. "A formal statement of morphenic analysis," *SIL* 10.27-39 (1952).

9 KOUTSOUDAS, Andreas. "The morpheme reconsidered," *IJAL* 29.160-70 (1963).

10 LANDAR, Herbert. "Reduplication and morphology," *Lang* 37.239-46 (1961).

11 NIDA, Eugene A. *Morphology: The Descriptive Analysis of Words,* 2d edition. Ann Arbor: Univ. of Michigan Press, 1949.*

12 SAPORTA, Sol. "Morph, morpheme, archimorpheme," *Word* 12.9-14 (1956).

13 SCHULTINK, H. "On word-identity," *Lingua* 11.354-62 (1962).

14 WELMERS, William E. "Tonemics, morphotonemics, and tonal morphemes," *GL* 4.1-9 (1958).

15 WINTER, Werner. "Form and meaning in linguistic analysis," *Linguistics* 3.5-18 (1964).

Phonemics

See also 2.8, and PHONEMICS, p. 51.

16 ANDRADE, M. J. "Some questions of fact and policy concerning phonemes," *Lang* 12.1-14 (1936).

17 BAZELL, C. E. "Three conceptions of phonological interpretation," *For Roman Jakobson* [5.16], 25-30.

18 BELASCO, Simon. "The differentiation of allophonic and nonallophonic segments in phonemic analysis," *AS* 34.269-79 (1959).

19 BLOCH, Bernard. "Phonemic overlapping," *AS* 16.278-84 (1941); Also in *Readings in Linguistics* [6.6], 93-96.

20 BLOCH, Bernard. "A set of postulates for phonemic analysis," *Lang.* 24.3-46 (1948).*

21 BOLINGER, Dwight L. "Ambiguities in pitch accent," *Word* 17.309-17 (1961).

22 BOLINGER, Dwight L. "Binomials and pitch accent," *Lingua* 11.34-44 (1962).

23 BOLINGER, Dwight L. "Contrastive accent and contrastive stress," *Lang* 37.83-96 (1961).

24 BOLINGER, Dwight L. "Intonation and grammar," *LL* 8.31-9 (1957).

1   BOLINGER, Dwight L. "Length, vowel, juncture," *Linguistics* 1.5-29 (1963).

2   CARROLL, John B. "The assessment of phoneme cluster frequencies," *Lang* 34.267-78 (1958).

3   CHAO, Yuen Ren. "On the non-uniqueness of phonemic analyses," *Bull. of the Institute of History and Philosophy*, Academia Sinica, 4.363-97 (1934). Also in *Readings in Linguistics* [6.6], 38-54.*

4   FISCHER-JØRGENSEN, Eli. "The phonetic basis for identification of phonemic elements," *JAS* 24.611-17; 25.576 (1952 and 1953).

5   FRIES, Charles C., and Kenneth L. PIKE. "Co-existent phonemic systems," *Lang* 25.29-50 (1949).*

6   HALLE, Morris. "The strategy of phonemics," *Word* 10.197-209 (1954).

7   HARARY, Frank, and Herbert H. PAPER. "Toward a general calculus of phonemic distribution," *Lang* 33.143-69 (1957).

8   HARRIS, Zellig S. "Simultaneous components in phonology," *Lang* 20.181-205 (1944); Also in *Readings in Linguistics* [6.6], 124-38.

9   HAUGEN, Einar. "Phoneme or prosodeme?" *Lang* 25.278-82 (1949).

10 HILL, Archibald A. "Phonetic and phonemic change," *Lang.* 12.15-22 (1936); Also in *Readings in Linguistics* [6.6], 81-4.

11 HILL, Archibald A. "Suprasegmentals, prosodies, prosodemes," *Lang* 37.457-68 (1961).

12 HOCKETT, Charles F. *A Manual of Phonology*. Baltimore: Williams and Wilkins, 1955. (*IJAL* 24:4 Pt. 1.)*

13 HOCKETT, Charles F. "Short and long syllable nuclei (with examples from Algonquian, Siouan, and Indo-European)," *IJAL* 19.165-71 (1953).

14 JONES, Daniel. *The Phoneme: Its Nature and Use*, 2nd edition. Cambridge, England: Heffer, 1962.*

15 KURATH, Hans. "Phonemics and phonics in historical phonology," *AS* 36.93-100 (1961). Also in *RAEL* [5.1], 262-69.

16 MARCHAND, James W. "Internal reconstruction of phonemic split," *Lang.* 32.245-53 (1956).

17 MARKEL, Norman N., and Eric P. HAMP. "Connotative meanings of certain phoneme sequences," *SIL* 15.47-61 (1961).

18 MOL, H. "On the phonetic description of the phoneme," *Lingua* 11.289-93 (1962).

19 MOL, H. "The relation between phonetics and phonemics—as one aspect of the 4th International Congress of Phonetic Sciences, Helsinki 1961 (I)," *Linguistics* 1.60-74 (1963).

20 MOL, H., and E. M. UHLENBECK. "Hearing and the concept of the phoneme," *Lingua* 8.161-85 (1959).

21 MOL, H., and E. M. UHLENBECK. "The linguistic relevance of intensity of stress," *Lingua* 2.205-13 (1949).

22 NIDA, Eugene A. "The identification of phonemes," *Lang* 24.414-41 (1948).

23 PERCIVAL, Keith. "A problem in competing phonemic solutions," *Lang* 36.383-86 (1960).

24 PETERSON, Gordon E., and Frank HARARY. "Foundations of phonemic theory," *Structure of Language* [6.5], 139-65.

25 PIKE, Kenneth L. "Grammatical prerequisites to phonemic analysis," *Word* 3.155-72 (1947); "More on grammatical prerequisites," *Word* 8.106-21 (1952).

1 PIKE, Kenneth L. *Phonemics: A Technique for Reducing Languages to Writing.* Ann Arbor: Univ. of Michigan Press, 1947.*

2 PIKE, Kenneth L. *Tone Languages: A Technique for Determining the Number and Type of Pitch Contrasts in a Language, with Studies in Tonemic Substitution and Fusion.* Ann Arbor: Univ. of Michigan Press, 1948.*

3 PIKE, Kenneth L., and Willard KINDBERG. "A problem in multiple stresses," *Word* 12.415-28 (1956).

4 POTTER, Simeon. "Syllabic juncture," *P4ICPS* [6.16], 728-31.

5 REICHLING, A. "Feature analysis and linguistic interpretation," *For Roman Jakobson* [5.16], 418-22.

6 SAPIR, Edward. "Sound patterns in language," *Lang* 1.37-51 (1925); Also in *Readings in Linguistics* [6.6], 19-25.

7 SØRENSEN, Holger Steen. "The phoneme and the phoneme variant," *Lingua* 9.68-88 (1960).

8 SWADESH, Morris. "The phonemic principle," *Lang* 10.117-29 (1934); Also in *Readings in Linguistics* [6.6], 32-7.*

9 SWADESH, Morris. "Twaddell on defining the phoneme," *Lang* 11.244-50 (1935).

10 SWADESH, Morris, and Charles F. VOEGELIN. "A problem in phonological alternation," *Lang* 15.1-10 (1939); Also in *Readings in Linguistics* [6.6], 88-92.

11 TRAGER, George L. "Some thoughts on 'juncture'," *SIL* 16.11-22 (1962).

12 TWADDELL, W. Freeman. "On defining the phoneme," *Lang. Monograph* 16 (1935); Also in *Readings in Linguistics* [6.6], 55-80.*

13 TWADDELL, W. Freeman. "Phonemes and allophones in speech analysis," *JAS* 24.607-11 (1952).

14 TWADDELL, W. Freeman. "Stetson's model and the 'Supra-Segmental Phonemes'," *Lang* 29.415-53 (1953).

15 VOEGELIN, C. F. "Linear phonemes and additive components," *Word* 12.429-43 (1956).

16 WIREN, Jacop, and Harold L. STUBBS. "Electronic binary selection system for phoneme classification," *JAS* 28.1082-91 (1956).

Phonetics

GENERAL

See also 6.7, 72.8, 72.17, and PHONETICS, p. 52.

17 ALBRIGHT, Erhard. *The International Phonetic Alphabet: Its Backgrounds and Development.* (PRCAFL no. 7) Bloomington, Ind.: Indiana Univ., 1958. [Issued also as Part III of *IJAL* 24:1.]

18 AUSTIN, William M. "Criteria for phonetic similarity," *Lang* 33.538-44 (1957).

19 AUSTIN, William M. "Phonotactics and the identity theorem," *SIL* 15.14-18 (1960).

20 BENTLEY, Madison, and Edith J. VARON. "An accessory study of 'phonetic symbolism'," *American Journal of Psychology* 14:1.76-86 (1933).

21 BOLINGER, Dwight L. "Around the edge of language: intonation," *HER* 34.282-96 (1964).

1 BOLINGER, Dwight L. "Intonation as a universal," *P9ICL* [6.15], 833-44 (1964).

2 BROSNAHAN, L. F. *The Sounds of Language: An Inquiry into the Role of Genetic Factors in the Development of Sound Systems*. Cambridge, Eng.: Heffer, 1961.

3 DANEŠ, František. "Sentence intonation from a functional point of view," *Word* 16.34-54 (1960).

4 DAVIS, T. K. "Sounds in language," *Journal of Nervous and Mental Diseases* 88.491-9 (1938). [Sound and symbolism.]

5 DE GROOT, A. Willem. "Phonetics in its relation to aesthetics," *Manual of Phonetics* [6.1], 385-400.

6 EISENSON, Jon. "A second study in the affective value of speech sounds," *QJS* 29.457-64 (1943).

7 FIRTH, John R. "Sounds and prosodies," *TPS* (1948), 127-52. Also in *Papers* [7.11], 121-8.

8 GRAY, Giles Wilkeson, and Claud Merton WISE. *The Bases of Speech*, 3rd edition. New York: Harper and Row, 1959.*

9 HAAS, William. "Relevance in phonetic analysis," *Word* 15.1-18 (1959).

10 HALLE, Morris. "Why and how do we study the sounds of speech?" *Report of the Fifth . . . Meeting on Linguistics and Language Teaching*, pp. 73-80. Washington: Georgetown Univ. Press, 1954.

11 HALLE, Morris, G. W. HUGHES, and J. P. A. RADLEY. "Acoustic properties of stop consonants," *JAS* 29.107-16 (1957).

12 HEFFNER, Roe-Merrill S. *General Phonetics*. Madison: Univ. of Wisconsin Press, 1952.*

13 JAKOBSON, Roman, and Morris HALLE. "Tenseness and laxness," *In Honour of Daniel Jones* [5.11], 96-101.

14 JOOS, Martin. *Acoustic Phonetics*. *Lang. Monograph* No. 23, 1948. Baltimore: Linguistic Society of America, 1948.*

15 KANTNER, Claude E., and Robert W. WEST. *Phonetics: An Introduction to the Principles of Phonetic Science from the Point of View of English Speech*. Rev. edition. New York: Harper and Row, 1960.*

16 KENYON, John S. "Need of a uniform phonetic alphabet," *QJS* 37.311-20 (1951).

17 KINGDON, Roger. "The representation of vowels," *In Honour of Daniel Jones* [5.11], 112-15.

18 NEWMAN, Edwin B. "Statistical methods in phonetics," *Manual of Phonetics* [6.7], 118-26.

19 O'CONNOR, J. D., and L. M. TRIM. "Vowel, consonant, syllable—a phonological definition," *Word* 9.103-22 (1953).

20 PAGET, Sir Richard. *Human Speech*. New York: Harcourt, Brace and World, 1930.

21 PETERS, Robert W. "Dimensions of perception for consonants," *JAS* 35.1985-90 (1963).

22 PIKE, Eunice V. "A test for predicting phonetic ability," *LL* 9.35-42 (1959).

23 PIKE, Kenneth L. *Phonetics: A Critical Analysis of Phonetic Theory and a Technic for the Practical Description of Sounds*. Ann Arbor: Univ. of Michigan Press, 1943.*

24 PIKE, Kenneth L. "Practical phonetics of rhythm waves," *Phonetica* 8.9-30 (1963).

1   POLITZER, Robert L. "Phonetics, phonemics, and pronunciation: theory," *Georgetown University Monograph Series on Languages and Linguistics,* No. 6, 19-27 (1954).

2   (*The*) *Principles of the International Phonetic Association, Being a Description of the International Phonetic Alphabet and the Manner of Using It, Illustrated by Texts in 51 Languages.* London: International Phonetic Association, Univ. College, 1949.*

3   STETSON, R. H. *Bases of Phonology.* Oberlin, Ohio: Oberlin College, 1945.*

4   SWEET, Henry. *A Handbook of Phonetics.* Oxford: Clarendon Press, 1877.*

5   TRAGER, George L. "The theory of accentual systems," *Language, Culture, and Personality* [7.1], 131-45.

6   WISE, C. M. *Applied Phonetics.* Englewood Cliffs, N.J.: Prentice-Hall, 1957.

EXPERIMENTAL

See also **6.7.**

7   BELASCO, Simon. "Influence of force of articulation of consonants on vowel duration," *JAS* 25.1015-16 (1953).

8   BLACK, John W. "Predicting the intelligibility of words," *P4ICPS* [6.16], 347-54 (1962).

9   BROWN, Roger, and Donald C. HILDUM. "Expectancy and the perception of syllables," *Lang* 32.411-19 (1956).

10   CASTLE, William E. *The Effect of Narrow-band Filtering on the Perception of Certain English Vowels (Janua Linguarum,* series Practica, 13) 's-Gravenhage: Mouton, 1964.

11   COHEN, A. "On the value of experimental phonetics for the linguist," *Lingua* 11.67-74 (1962).

12   CURRY, E. T. "An experimental study of the relative identification thresholds of nine American vowels," *SM* 17.90-94 (1950).

13   DELATTRE, Pierre. "Classifying speech sounds by their source," *In Honour of Daniel Jones* [5.11], 46-52.

14   DELATTRE, Pierre. "The physiological interpretation of sound spectrograms," *PMLA* 66.864-75 (1951).

15   DELATTRE, Pierre. "Quality in tape recording and voicing," *IJAL* 29.55-60 (1963).

16   DENES, Peter B. "On the statistics of spoken English," *JAS* 35.892-904 (1963).

17   DENES, Peter B., and Elliot N. PINSON. *The Speech Chain: The Physics and Biology of Spoken Language.* Baltimore: Williams and Wilkins, 1963.

18   FIRTH, John R. "Linguistics in the laboratory," *ZPAS* 12.27-35 (1959; pub. 1961).

19   FISCHER-JØRGENSEN, Eli. "What can the new techniques of acoustic phonetics contribute to linguistics?" *P8ICL* [6.15], 433-78 (1958).

20   FRY, Dennis B. "Experimental evidence for the phoneme," *In Honour of Daniel Jones* [5.11], 59-72.

21   FRY, Dennis B. "Perception and recognition in speech," *For Roman Jakobson* [5.16], 169-73.

22   FRY, Dennis B. "The perception of stress," *P8ICL* [6.15], 601-3 (1958).

23   GOFORTH, John L. "Speech stretcher for language studies," *Electronics* 24:12.94-7 (1951).

1 GREEN, P. S. "Consonant-vowel transitions," *SL* 12.57-105 (1958).

2 HANLEY, T. D. "An analysis of vocal intensity and duration characteristics of selected samples of speech from three American dialect regions," *SM* 18.78-93 (1951).

3 HARRIS, K. S. "Cues for the discrimination of American English fricatives in spoken syllables," *L&S* 1.1-8 (1958).

4 HERDAN, G. "The relation between the functional burdening of phonemes and their frequency of occurrence," *L&S* 1.8-14 (1958).

5 HIBBITT, G. W. *Diphthongs in American Speech: A Study of the Duration of Diphthongs in the Contextual Speech of Two Hundred and Ten Male Undergraduates.* (Diss.) New York: Columbia Univ. Press, 1948.

6 HOUSE, Arthur S. "On vowel duration in English," *JAS* 33.1174-8 (1961).

7 JOOS, Martin. "The definition of juncture and terminals," *Second Texas Conference* [13.24], 4-23.

8 KOPP, G. A., and H. C. GREEN. "Basic phonetic principles of visible speech," *JAS* 18.74-89 (1946).

9 LADEFOGED, Peter. *Elements of Acoustic Phonetics.* Chicago: Univ. of Chicago Press, 1962.

10 LEHISTE, Ilse. *An Acoustic-Phonetic Study of Open Juncture.* Suppl. to *Phonetica* 5, 1960.

11 LEHISTE, Ilse, and G. E. PETERSON. "Transitions, glides, and diphthongs," *JAS* 33.268-77 (1961).

12 LIBERMAN, A. M., K. S. HARRIS, H. S. HOFFMAN, and B. C. GRIFFITH. "The discrimination of speech sounds within and across phoneme boundaries," *Journal of Experimental Psychology* 54.358-68 (1957).

13 LIBERMAN, Philip. "Some acoustical correlates of word stress in American English," *JAS* 32.451-4 (1960).

14 LISKER, Leigh. "Closure duration and the intervocalic voiced-voiceless distinction in English," *Lang* 33.42-9 (1957).

15 LISKER, Leigh. "The distinction between [æ] and [ɛ]: a problem in acoustic analysis," *Lang* 24.397-407 (1948).

16 LISKER, Leigh, Franklin S. COOPER, and Alvin M. LIBERMAN. "The uses of experiment in language description," *Word* 18.82-106 (1962).

17 MILLER, George A., and Patricia E. NICELY. "An analysis of perceptual confusions among some English consonants," *JAS* 27.338-52, 617 (1955).

18 NEWMAN, Stanley S. "Further experiments in phonetic symbolism," *American Journal of Psychology* 14:1.53-75 (1933).

19 PETERSON, Gordon E. "Phonetics, phonemics, and pronunciation: spectrographic analysis," *Georgetown University Monograph Series on Languages and Linguistics,* No. 6, 7-18 (1954).

20 PETERSON, Gordon E., and Ilse LEHISTE. "Duration of syllable nuclei in English," *JAS* 32.693-703 (1960).

21 PETERSON, Gordon E., and M. S. COXE. "The vowels [e] and [o] in American speech," *QJS* 29.33-41 (1953).

22 PIERCE, Joe E. "Spectrographic study of vocalic nuclei," *LL* 12:3.241-7 (1962).

23 POTTER, Ralph K., G. A. KOPP, and H. C. GREEN. *Visible Speech.* New York: Van Nostrand, 1947.*

26

1 Pulgram, Ernst. *Introduction to the Spectrography of Speech.* (*Janua Linguarum,* 7). 's-Gravenhage: Mouton, 1959.*

2 Russell, G. Oscar. *The Vowel.* Columbus: The Ohio State Univ. Press, 1928.*

3 Sharf, Donald J. "Duration of post-stress intervocalic stops and preceding vowels," *L&S* 5.26-30 (1962).

4 Shoup, J. E. "Phoneme selection for studies in automatic speech recognition," *JAS* 34.397-403 (1962).

5 Solomon, Lawrence N. "Semantic approach to the perception of complex sounds," *JAS* 30.421-5 (1958).

6 Stetson, R. H. *Motor Phonetics, A Study of Speech Movements in Action,* rev. ed. Oberlin, Ohio, 1951.*

7 Stowe, Arthur N., William P. Harris, and Donald B. Hampton. "Signal and context components of word-recognition behavior," *JAS* 35.639-44 (1963).

8 Trager, Edith Crowell. "Vowel recognition by computer: a report and critique," *SIL* 15.8-13 (1960).

9 Wang, William S-Y, and John Crawford. "Frequency studies of English consonants," *L&S* 3.131-9 (1960).

Historical (Phonology)

See also 1.16, and Historical Grammar, p. 41, Old English, p. 42, Middle English, p. 43, and Early Modern English, p. 47.

10 Collinge, N. E. "The limitations of historical phonology," *ArL* 8.111-28 (1956).

11 Dyen, Isidore. "Why phonetic change is regular," *Lang* 39.631-7 (1963).

12 Hoenigswald, Henry M. "Diachronic soundcharts: a technique to represent soundchange," *SIL* 6.81-94 (1948).

13 Joos, Martin. "The medieval sibilants," *Lang* 28.222-31 (1952). Repr. in *Readings in Linguistics* [6.6], 372-78.

14 Ladd, Charles A. "The nature of sound-change," *P9ICL* [6.15], 650-57.

15 Lehman, Winfred P. "Types of sound-change," *P9ICL* [6.15], 658-62.

16 Penzl, Herbert. "The evidence for phonemic changes," *Whatmough Festschrift* [6.17], 193-208.

17 Penzl, Herbert. "Orthographic evidence for types of phonemic change," *P8ICL* [6.15], 119-43.

18 Prins, A. A. "Historical phonology and phonetic theory," *Museum* 63.161-74 (1958).

Psycholinguistics; the Psychology of Language

See also 6.19, 74.16, 75.6, 75.10, 83.14, 87.23, and 88.6.

19 Ballard, Philip B. *Thought and Language.* London: Univ. of London Press, 1934.

20 Bloomer, R. H. "Level of abstraction as a function of modifier load," *Journal of Educational Research* 52.269-72 (1959).

21 Bolinger, Dwight L. "Thoughts on 'yep' and 'nope'!" *AS* 21.90-95 (1946).

22 Bolinger, Dwight L. "Verbal evocation," *Lingua* 10.113-27 (1961).

23 Brown, Roger. *Words and Things.* Glencoe, Ill.: The Free Press, 1958.*

24 Brown, Roger, and Don E. Dulaney. "A stimulus-response analysis of language and meaning," *Language, Thought, and Culture* [6.2], 49-95.

LINGUISTICS

1 BROWN, Roger, and Marguerite FORD. "Address in American English," *Journal of Abnormal and Social Psychology* 62.375-85 (1961). Also in *Language in Culture and Society* [6.3], 234-44.

2 BRYANT, Margaret M., and Janet AIKEN. *Psychology of English; Why We Say What We Do,* Rev. ed. New York: Frederick Ungar, 1962.

3 CARROLL, John B. "Words, meanings, and concepts," *HER* 34.178-202 (1964).

4 CHOMSKY, Noam. "Review of B. F. Skinner: *Verbal Behavior,*" *Lang.* 35.26-58 (1959).*

5 ERVIN-TRIPP, Susan. "An analysis of the interaction of language, topic, and listener," *Ethnography* [5.15], 86-102.

6 GALT, William. "Our mother tongue; etymological implications of the social neurosis," *Psychoanalytical Review* 30.241-62 (1943).

7 GOLDMAN-EISLER, Frieda. "Speech production and the predictability of words in context," *Quart. Jrnl. of Exp. Psych.* 10.96-106 (1958).

8 GOLDSTEIN, Kurt. "On naming and pseudo-naming from experiences in psychopathology," *Word* 2.1-7 (1946).

9 HARGAN, James. "The psychology of prison language," *JASP* 30.359-65 (1935).

10 JENKINS, James J. "Commonality of association as an indicator of more general patterns of verbal behavior," *Style in Language* [6.20], 307-29.

11 McGRANAHAN, D. V. "The psychology of language," *Psych. Bulletin* 31.178-216 (1936). [Bib.]

12 MILLER, George A. "The perception of speech," *For Roman Jakobson* [5.16], 353-60.

13 NEWMAN, Edwin B. "The pattern of vowels and consonants in various languages," *Amer. Jrnl. of Psych.* 64.367-79 (1951).

14 OLMSTED, David L., and Omar Khayyam MOORE. "Language, psychology and linguistics," *Psychological Review* 59.414-20 (1952).

15 OSGOOD, Charles E. "Some effects of motivation on style of encoding," *Style in Language* [6.20], 293-306.

16 OSGOOD, Charles E., and Thomas A. SEBEOK, eds. *Psycholinguistics: A Survey of Theory and Research Problems,* incl. A. Richard Diebold, Jr., *A Survey of Psycholinguistic Research 1954–64.* Second edition. Bloomington, Ind.: Indiana Univ. Press, 1965.

17 OSGOOD, Charles E., George J. SUCI, and Percy H. TANNENBAUM. *The Measurement of Meaning.* Urbana, Ill.: Univ. of Illinois Press, 1957.

18 PILLSBURY, Walter B., and Clarence L. MEADER. *The Psychology of Language.* New York: Appleton-Century-Crofts, 1928.

19 PITTENGER, Robert E., and Henry Lee SMITH, Jr. "A basis for some contributions of linguistics to Psychiatry," *Psychiatry: Journal for the Study of Interpersonal Processes* 20:1.61-78 (1957).

20 *Proceedings of the Second Conference on Verbal Learning and Verbal Behavior,* June 1961, Charles N. Cofer and Barbara S. Musgrave, eds. New York: McGraw-Hill, 1963.

21 PRONKO, N. H. "Language and psycholinguistics: a review," *Psych. Bull.* 43.189-239 (1946).

22 REICHARD, Gladys A., Roman JAKOBSON, and Elizabeth WERTH. "Language and synesthesia," *Word* 5.224-33 (1949). [Sound symbolism.]

28 LINGUISTICS

1 ROBACK, A. A. *Destiny and Motivation in Language: Studies in Psycho-linguistics and Glossodynamics.* Cambridge, Mass.: Sci-Art Publishers, 1954.

2 SCHLAGEL, Richard H. "Language and perception," *PPR* 23.192-204 (1962).

3 SKINNER, B. F. *Verbal Behavior.* New York: Appleton-Century-Crofts, 1957.*

4 SOLOMON, Richard L., and H. Howes DAVIS. "Word frequency, personal values, and visual thresholds," *Psychological Review* 63.256-70 (1951).

5 STEIN, Martin H. "The cliché: a phenomenon of resistance," *Journal of the American Psychoanalytical Assoc.* 6.263-77 (1958).

6 USHENKO, Andrew Paul. *The Field Theory of Meaning.* Ann Arbor: Univ. of Michigan Press, 1958.

7 WERNER, Heinz, and Edith KAPLAN. "Development of word meaning through verbal context: an experimental study," *Journal of Psychology* 29.251-7 (1950).

8 ZIPF, George Kingsley. "The meaning frequency relationship of words," *Journal of General Psych.* 33.251-6 (1945).

9 ZIPF, George Kingsley. *The Psycho-Biology of Language.* Boston: Houghton Mifflin, 1935.

Semantics: Language and Philosophy

GENERAL

See also **5.18, 6.1, 34.19, 84.12, 84.20, 84.25, 85.2,** and *Taboo . . .*, p. **87.**

10 ALSTON, William P. "Philosophical analysis and structural linguistics," *JP* 59.709-20 (1962).

11 ANTAL, László. "Sign, meaning, context," *Lingua* 10.211-19 (1961).

12 AYER, Alfred J. *Language, Truth, and Logic.* London: Gollancz, 1936.*

13 BERGMAN, Gustav. "Two types of linguistic philosophy," *The Review of Metaphysics* 5.417-38 (1952).

14 BLACK, Max. *Models and Metaphors: Studies in Language and Philosophy.* Ithaca, N.Y.: Cornell Univ. Press, 1962.

15 BRIN, Joseph G. *Applied Semantics.* Boston: Bruce Humphries, 1951.

16 BURKE, Kenneth. *A Grammar of Motives.* New York: Prentice-Hall, 1945.

17 CARNAP, Rudolf. *Introduction to Semantics.* Cambridge: Harvard Univ. Press, 1942.*

18 CARNAP, Rudolf. *Logical Syntax of Language.* New York: Harcourt, Brace and World, 1937.*

19 CARNAP, Rudolph. *Meaning and Necessity: A Study in Semantics and Modal Logic,* 2nd ed., enl. Chicago: Univ. of Chicago Press, 1956.

20 CASSIRER, Ernst. "The influence of language upon the development of scientific thought," *JP* 39.309-327 (1942).

21 CASSIRER, Ernst. *Language and myth.* New York: Harper and Row, 1946.*

22 CHOMSKY, Noam. "Logical syntax and semantics: their linguistic relevance," *Lang* 31.36-45 (1955). Cf. Bar-Hillel [**12.4**].

23 DeLAGUNA, Grace A. "Communication, the act, and the object with reference to Mead," *JP* 43.225-38 (1946).

1 EMPSON, William. *The Structure of Complex Words*. Norfolk, Conn.: New Directions, 1951.

2 GORMAN, Margaret, R.S.C.J. *General Semantics and Contemporary Thomism*. Lincoln: Univ. of Nebraska Press, 1962. [Bison 146.]

3 HAYAKAWA, S. I. *Language in Thought and Action*. 2d ed. New York: Harcourt, Brace and World, 1964.

4 HAYAKAWA, S. I. "The semantics of being Negro," *ETC*. 10.163-75 (1953).

5 JACOBS, Wilhelmina, and Vivian JACOBS. "The color blue: its use as metaphor and symbol," *AS* 33.29-46 (1958).

6 KAPLAN, Abraham. "Content analysis and the theory of signs," *Philosophy of Science* 10.230-47 (1943).

7 KEENE, G. B. *Language and Reasoning*. London and New York: Van Nostrand, 1961.

8 KLUCKHOHN, Clyde. "General semantics and 'primitive' languages," *General Semantics Bull.*, Nos. 20 and 21, 24-30 (1957). [Alfred Korzybski memorial lecture.]

9 KORZYBSKI, Alfred. *Science and Sanity*, 2d edition. Lancaster, Pa.: Science Press, 1941.*

10 LANGER, Suzanne. *Philosophy in a New Key*. New York: New American Library, 1959.* [Ment MP475.]

11 LASSWELL, Harold D., *et al. Language of Politics; Studies in Quantitative Semantics*. New York: G. W. Stewart, 1949.

12 LEE, Irving J., ed. *The Language of Wisdom and Folly. Background Readings in Semantics*. New York: Harper & Bros., 1949.

13 LEHNER, Ernst. *Symbols, Signs and Signets*. Cleveland: World Publishing Co., 1950.

14 LENNEBERG, Eric H., and J. M. ROBERTS. *The Language of Experience. IJAL*, vol. 24, suppl. (1956).

15 LINSKY, Leonard, ed. *Semantics and the Philosophy of Language: A Collection of Readings*. Urbana: Univ. of Illinois Press, 1952.

16 LONGABAUGH, Theodore. *General Semantics: An Introduction*. New York: Vantage Press, 1957.

17 MacMURRAY, John. "The analysis of language," *PhQ* 1.319-37 (1951).

18 MALONEY, Martin. "General semantics and linguistics: some similarities and differences," *General Semantics Bull.*, Nos. 8-9.57-62, 70 (1952).

19 MATES, Benson. "Synonymity," *UCP in Philosophy* 25.201-26 (1950). Also in Linsky [**29**.15].

20 MORRIS, Charles. *Signs, Language, and Behavior*. New York: Prentice-Hall, 1946. Repr. New York: Braziller, 1955.*

21 NESBIT, Frank F. *Language, Meaning and Reality*. New York: Exposition Press, 1955.

22 NEUMANN, Joshua H. "Coleridge on the English language," *PMLA* 63.642-61 (1948).

23 OGDEN, Charles K., and I. A. RICHARDS. *The Meaning of Meaning*. New York: Harcourt, Brace and World, 3d ed., rev., 1930.*

24 PAP, Arthur. *Semantics and Necessary Truth: An Inquiry into the Foundations of Analytic Philosophy*. New Haven, Conn.: Yale Univ. Press, 1958.

1 PHILBRICK, F. A. *Language and the Law; The Semantics of Forensic English.* New York: Macmillan, 1951.

2 QUINE, William Van Orman. *Word and Object.* Cambridge, Mass.: M.I.T. Press; and New York: Wiley, 1964.

3 RENWICK, Ralph, Jr. "Seventeenth-century semantics," *ETC.* 19:1.85-93 (1962).

4 RICHARDS, Ivor A. *Speculative Instruments.* London: Routledge and Kegan Paul, 1955. [Theory of language.]

5 STEVENSON, C. L. *Ethics and Language.* New Haven: Yale Univ. Press, 1945. [Yale Y-19.]*

6 STOLL, Elmer E. "Critics at cross-purposes," *ELH* 14.320-8 (1947).

7 STORER, Thomas. "Linguistic isomorphisms," *Philosophy of Science* 19.77-85 (1952).

8 URBAN, W. M. *Language and Reality: The Philosophy of Language and the Principles of Symbolism.* London: Allen and Unwin, 1939.*

9 WEINBERG, H. L. *Levels of Knowing and Existence; Studies in General Semantics.* New York: Harper and Row, 1959.

10 WERNER, Heinz, and Bernard KAPLAN. *Symbol Formation: An Organismic-developmental Approach to Language and the Expression of Thought.* New York: Wiley, 1963.

11 WHITEHEAD, Alfred North. *Symbolism, Its Meaning and Effect.* New York: Macmillan, 1927. [Cap. 13]

LINGUISTIC (SEMASIOLOGY)

See also 2.17, 27.17, 28.7-8, 34.14, 79.21, 80.11, 86.23, 88.22, and *Taboo . . . ,* p. 87.

12 ALLEN, Robert L. "The structure of meaning," *P9ICL* [6.15], 421-26.

13 ANTAL, László. "Meaning and its change," *Linguistics* 6.14-28 (1964).

14 BAZELL, C. E. "Meaning and the morpheme," *Word* 18.132-42 (1962).

15 BERKNER, S. S. "On the interplay of English dialogue utterances," *ZAA* 10.203-12 (1962).

16 BLAKE, Frank R. "A study of language from the semantic point of view," *IF* 56:4.241-55 (1938).

17 BOLINGER, Dwight L. "The life and death of words," *ASch* 22.323-35 (1953).

18 BRÉAL, Michel. *Semantics: Studies in the Science of Meaning,* trans. Mrs. Henry Cust. London: Heinemann, 1900.*

19 BUCK, Carl D. "Words for world, earth and land, sun," *Lang* 5.215-27 (1929).

20 CHARLESTON, Britta M. *Studies on the Emotional and Affective Means of Expression in Modern English.* (Schweitzer Anglistische Arbeiten, Vol. 46.) Bern: Franke, 1960.

21 COLLITZ, Klara H. *Verbs of Motion in Their Semantic Divergence. Lang Monographs,* No. 8. Philadelphia Linguistic Society of America, 1931.

22 COPLEY, J. *Shift of Meaning.* London: Oxford Univ. Press, 1961.

23 CULBERT, Sidney S. "Perceptual distortion resulting from semantic transfer: a study in verbal mediation," *SL* 8.77-81 (1954).

24 EATON, Helen S. *Semantic Frequency List for English, French, German and Spanish.* Chicago: Chicago Univ. Press, 1940. [Review, G. K. Lipfin, *AS* 16.43-5 (1941).]

LINGUISTICS **31**

1 EBELING, Carl. "Phonemics and functional semantics," *Lingua* 3.309-21 (1953).

2 ERVIN, Susan M. "The connotations of gender," *Word* 18.248-61 (1962).

3 FIRTH, John R. "The technique of semantics," *TPS*, 1935, 36-72; also in *Papers in Linguistics* [7.12], 7-33.

4 FUNKE, Otto. "On some synchronic problems of semantics," *ES* 34.258-61 (1953).

5 GARVIN, Paul L. "A descriptive technique for the treatment of meaning," *Lang* 34.1-32 (1958).

6 GOODENOUGH, Ward H. "Componential analysis and the study of meaning," *Lang* 32.195-216 (1956).

7 HAAS, William. "Semantic value." *P9ICL* [6.15], 1066-72 (1964).

8 HEILMANN, Luigi. "Statistical considerations and semantic content," *P9ICL* [6.15], 427-32 (1964).

9 HILL, Archibald A. "Linguistic principles for interpreting meaning," *CE* 22.466-73 (1961).

10 HOUSEHOLDER, Fred W. "On the uniqueness of semantic mapping," *Word* 18.173-85 (1962).

11 JOOS, Martin. "Semology: a linguistic theory of meaning," *SIL* 13.53-70 (1958).*

12 KATZ, Jerrold J., and Jerry A. FODOR. "The structure of a semantic theory," *Lang* 39.170-210 (1963).*

13 KROEBER, A. L. "Semantic contribution of lexicostatistics," *IJAL* 27.1-8 (1961).

14 KROESCH, Samuel. "Semantic borrowing in Old English," *Klaeber Miscellany* [6.10], 50-72.

15 LEISI, Ernst. "The problem of the 'hard words'," *ES* 34.262-7 (1953).

16 LEPLEY, William M., and John L. KOBRICK. "Word usage and synonym representation in the English language," *JASP* 47, Supplement, 572-3 (1952).

17 LEVIN, Samuel R. "Aspects of semantic and grammatical change," *Linguistics* 2.26-37 (1963).

18 LOUNSBURY, Floyd G. *The Varieties of Meaning.* Georgetown Univ. Monograph Series on Languages and Linguistics, No. 4. Washington, D.C., 1953.

19 MALONE, Kemp. "Anglo-Saxon: a semantic study," *RES* 5.173-85 (1929).

20 MENNER, Robert J. "Multiple meaning and change of meaning in English," *Lang* 21.59-76 (1945).

21 NEWMAN, Stanley S. "Semantic problems in grammatical systems and lexemes: a search for method," *Language in Culture* [33.13], 82-91.

22 NIDA, Eugene A. "A system for the description of semantic elements," *Word* 7.1-14 (1951).

23 NOYES, Gertrude E. "The beginnings of the study of synonyms in England," *PMLA* 66.951-70 (1951).

24 PIMSLEUR, Paul. "Semantic frequency counts," *MT* 4.11-13 (1957).

25 READ, Allen Walker. "An account of the word 'semantics'," *Word* 4.78-97 (1948).

1 REIFLER, Erwin. "A few striking examples demonstrating the contribution comparative semasiology can make towards historical linguistics," *P8ICL*, 1958 [6.14], 622-25.

2 REIFLER, Erwin. "Linguistic analysis and comparative semantics," *ETC.* 12.33-6 (1954).

3 ROBINS, R. H. "A problem in the statement of meanings," *Lingua* 3.121-37 (1952).

4 RUDSKOGER, Arne. *Fair, Foul, Nice, Proper: A Contribution to the Study of Polysemy.* GSE 1. Stockholm: Almqvist and Wiksell, 1952.

5 SALMON, Vivian. "Some connotations of 'cold' in Old and Middle English," *MLN* 74.314-22 (1959).

6 SCHIBSBYE, K. "The grammatical aspects of semantics," *ES* 40.455-8 (1959).

7 SCHREUDER, H. "On some cases of restriction of meaning," *ES* 37.117-24 (1956).

8 SMIT, J. "The theory of lexical semantics," *AUMLA* 16.179-87 (1961).

9 STERN, Gustav. *Meaning and Change of Meaning, with Special Reference to the English Language* (Göteborgs högskolas årsskrift 38). Göteborg: Elanders Boktryckeri Aktiebolag, 1931; repr. Bloomington: Indiana Univ. Press, 1963.*

10 SWAEN, A. E. H. "The palette set," *ES* 7.62-88 (1940). [On color names.]

11 THORNDIKE, E. L. "On the frequency of semantic changes in modern English," *Journal of General Psych.* 39.23-27 (1948).

12 ULLMANN, Stephen. "Descriptive semantics and linguistic typology," *Word* 9.225-40 (1953).

13 ULLMANN, Stephen. *Semantics: An Introduction to the Science of Meaning.* New York: Barnes & Noble, 1962. [Bib.]*

14 WHITE, Alan R. "Synonymous expressions," *PhQ* 8.193-207 (1958).

15 ZIFF, Paul. *Semantic Analysis.* Ithaca: Cornell Univ. Press, 1960.

Sociolinguistics; Language and Culture

See also 2.4, 66.15, 69.18, 73.3, 73.18-19-20, 79.17, 80.20, 82.7, 83.9, 83.19, and 83.22.

16 AKHMANOVA, Olga S. "Sociolinguistic variation in modern English," *CAn* 2.269 (1961).

17 BERNSTEIN, Basil. "Elaborate and restricted codes," *Ethnography* [5.15], 55-69.

18 BLACK, Max. "Linguistic relativity: the views of Benjamin Lee Whorf," *PhR* 78.228-38 (1963).

19 BOAS, Franz. *Race, Language and Culture.* New York: Macmillan, 1940. [Reprinted in paperback, The Free Press, Glencoe, Ill., 1966.] *

20 BRAM, Joseph. *Language and Society.* New York: Doubleday, 1955 [RH ss8].

21 BROWN, James Cooke. "Loglan," *Scientific American* 202.53-63 (1960). [Testing the Whorfian hypothesis.]

22 BROWN, Roger. "Linguistic determinism and the part of speech," *JASP* 55.1-5 (1957).

23 BRUTYAN, G. A. "A Marxist evaluation of the Whorf hypothesis," *ETC.* 19:2.199-220 (1962). [Tr. by Anatol Rapoport.]

24 CARROLL, John B. *Language and Thought.* Englewood Cliffs, N.J.: Prentice-Hall, 1964.*

1 COHEN, Marcel. "Social and linguistic structure," *Diogenes* 13.38-47 (1956).

2 CONKLIN, Harold C. "Linguistic play in its cultural context," *Lang* 35.631-6 (1959).

3 COUILLARD, Louis E. "The role of languages in the development of national consciousness: the Canadian experience," *PMLA* 72.43-8 (1957).

4 CURRIE, Haver C. "A projection of socio-linguistics: the relationship of speech to social status," *SSJ* 18.28-37 (1952).

5 DRAKE, James A. "The effect of urbanization on regional vocabulary," *AS* 36.17-33 (1961).

6 DRYSDALE, Patrick. "Language and culture," *QQ* 67.268-78 (1960).

7 FEARING, Franklin. "An examination of the conceptions of Benjamin Whorf in the light of theories of perception and cognition," *Language in Culture* [6.3], 47-81.

8 FISCHER, John L. "Social influences in the choice of a linguistic variant," *Word* 14.47-56 (1958). Also in *RAEL* [5.1], 307-315.

9 GREENBERG, Joseph H. "Concerning inferences from linguistic to nonlinguistic data," *Language in Culture* [6.3], 3-19.

10 GUMPERZ, John J. "Linguistic and social interaction in two communities," *Ethnography* [5.15], 137-53.

11 HALL, Edward T. "Adumbration as a feature of intercultural communication," *Ethnography* [5.15], 154-63.

12 HOCKETT, Charles F. "Language study and cultural attitudes," *LingR* 1:5.1,4-6 (1959).

13 HOIJER, Harry, ed. *Language in Culture. Proceedings of a Conference on the Interrelations of Language and Other Aspects of Culture.* Comp. Studies of Cultures and Civs., No. 3, Robert Redfield and Milton Singer, eds. Issued as *AA* 56:6 Pt. 2 (1954).

14 HORMANN, Bernhard L. "Hawaii's linguistic situation; a sociological interpretation in the new key," *Social Process in Hawaii* 24.6-31 (1960).

15 HORNE, Kibbey M. "Graphic representation of social isoglosses," *AnL* 6.1-9 (1964).

16 HYMES, Dell. "Toward ethnographies of communication," *Ethnography* [5.15], 1-34.

17 IVES, Sumner. "Use of field materials in the determination of dialect groupings," *QJS* 41.359-64 (1955).

18 JESPERSEN, Otto. *Mankind, Nation, and Individual from a Linguistic Point of View.* London: Allen and Unwin, 1946. [Midland MB 46.]*

19 LABOV, William. "Phonological correlates of social stratification," *Ethnography* [5.15], 164-76.

20 LAWTON, Denis. "Social class language differences in group discussion," *L&S* 7.183-204 (1964).

21 LENNEBERG, Eric H. "Cognition in ethnolinguistics," *Lang* 29.463-71 (1953).

22 LEWIS, M. M. *Language in Society.* New York: Social Sciences, Pubs., 1948.

23 McDAVID, Raven I., Jr. "American social dialects," *CE* 26.254-60 (1965).

24 McDAVID, Raven I., Jr. "Dialect differences and inter-group tensions," *SIL* 9.27-33 (1951).

1 McDavid, Raven I., Jr. "Social differences in pronunciation: a problem in methodology," *GL* 2.15-21 (1956).

2 McQuown, Norman A. "Analysis of the cultural content of language materials," *Language in Culture* [6.3], 82-91.

3 Menefee, Selden C. "The effect of stereotyped words on political judgments," *American Sociological Review* 1.614-21 (1936).

4 Newman, Stanley S. "Behavior patterns in linguistic structure: a case study," *Language, Culture, and Personality* [7.1], 94-106.

5 Nida, Eugene A. "Field techniques in descriptive linguistics," *IJAL* 13.138-46 (1947).

6 Pederson, Lee A. "Non-standard Negro speech in Chicago," *Non-Standard Speech and the Teaching of English,* ed. by William A. Stewart. Washington: Center for Applied Linguistics, 16-23 (1964).

7 Pieris, Ralph. "Speech and society: a sociological approach to language," *American Sociological Review* 16.499-505 (1951).

8 Pike, Kenneth L. *Language in Relation to a Unified Theory of the Structure of Human Behavior.* Glendale, Calif.: Summer Institute of Linguistics, Pt. 1, 1954; Pt. 2, 1955; Pt. 3, 1960.*

9 Putnam, George N., and Edna M. O'Hern. *The Status Significance of an Isolated Urban Dialect.* Lang. Diss. 53, Supplement to *Lang.* 1955.

10 Reed, David W. "Establishing and evaluating social boundaries in English," *Fries Studies* [6.11], 241-48.

11 Ross, Alan S. C. "U and Non-U," in Nancy Mitford, ed.: *Noblesse Oblige.* London: Hamish Hamilton, 1956.

12 Samora, Julian, and William N. Deane. "Language usage as a possible index of acculturation," *Sociology and Social Research* 40.307-11 (1956).

13 Sapir, Edward. *Culture, Language, and Personality; Selected Essays,* David G. Mandelbaum, ed. Berkeley: Univ. of California Press, 1956.

14 Shlien, John M. "Mother-in-law: a problem in kinship terminology," *ETC.* 19:2.161-71 (1962).

15 Söderlind, Johannes. "The attitude to language expressed by or ascertainable from English writers of the 16th and 17th centuries," *SN* 36.111-26 (1964).

16 Sommerfelt, Alf. "The interrelationship between language and culture," *TSLL* 1.449-56 (1960).

17 Trager, George L., and Edward T. Hall, Jr. "Culture and communication: a model and an analysis," *Explorations* 3.137-49 (1954).

18 Vossler, Karl. *The Spirit of Language in Civilization,* trans. by Oscar Oeser. London: K. Paul, Trench, Trübner, 1932.

19 Williams, Hazel Browne. "A semantic study of some current, pejoratively regarded language symbols involving Negroes in the United States: an approach to intergroup conflict through a study of language behavior," *General Semantics Bulletin,* No. 16 & 17, 26-34 (1955).

Structural Comparison, Comparative Linguistics, and Typology

See also 1.11, 27.13, 38.9, 38.12, 38.14-15, 38.19, 38.21-22-23, 38.25, 39.9, 39.13-14, and 39.21.

20 Abe, Isamu. "Intonational patterns of English and Japanese," *Word* 11.386-98 (1955).

1 ALLEN, W. Sidney. "Phonetics and comparative linguistics," *ArL* 3.126-36 (1951).

2 ALLEN, W. Sidney. "Relationship in comparative linguistics," *TPS* 1953.52-112.

3 BOLINGER, Dwight L. "English prosodic stress and Spanish sentence order," *Hispania* 37.152-6 (1954).

4 BOWEN, J. Donald. "A comparison of the intonation patterns of English and Spanish," *Hispania* 39.30-35 (1956).

5 COLLINSON, W. E. "Tradition and divergence in the syntax of some western languages," *TPS* (1959). 1-13.

6 COWAN, H. K. J. "A note on statistical methods in comparative linguistics," *Lingua* 8.233-46 (1959).

7 CURME, George O. "The forms and functions of the subjunctive in the classical and modern languages," *MP* 26.387-99 (1929).

8 DELATTRE, Pierre. "Comparing the prosodic features of English, German, Spanish and French," *IRAL* 1.193-210 (1963).

9 ELLIS, J. "General linguistics and comparative philology," *Lingua* 7.134-74 (1958).

10 GLEASON, H. A., Jr. "Comparison of linguistic systems," *IJAL* 22.273-5 (1956).

11 GREENBERG, Joseph H. "Is the vowel-consonant dichotomy universal?" *Word* 18.73-81 (1962).

12 GREENBERG, Joseph H. "The nature and uses of linguistic typologies," *IJAL* 23.68-77 (1957).

13 GREENBERG, Joseph H. "A quantitative approach to the morphological typology of language," *IJAL* 26.178-94 (1960).

14 HALL, Robert A., Jr. "The reconstruction of Proto-Romance," *Lang* 26.6-27 (1950). Also in *Readings in Linguistics* [6.6], 303-14.

15 HERDAN, Gustav. "The numerical expression of selective variation in the vowel-consonant sequence in English and Russian," *Whatmough Studies* [6.17], 91-104.

16 HOENIGSWALD, Henry M. *Language Change and Linguistic Reconstruction.* Chicago: Univ. of Chicago Press, 1960.*

17 HOENIGSWALD, Henry M. "The principal step in comparative grammar," *Lang* 26.357-64 (1950). Also in *Readings in Linguistics* [6.6], 298-302.

18 HOENIGSWALD, Henry M. "Some uses of nothing," *Lang* 35.409-21 (1959).

19 JAKOBSON, Roman. "Typological studies and their contribution to historical comparative linguistics," *P8ICL* [6.15], 17-35.

20 KAHANE, Henry R. "Principles of comparative syntax," *Orbis* 3.513-16 (1954).

21 KLEINJANS, Everett. "A comparison of Japanese and English object structures," *LL* 8.47-52 (1958).

22 KRÁMSKÝ, Jiří. "A quantitative typology of languages," *L&S* 2.72-85 (1959).

23 KUFNER, Herbert L. *The Grammatical Structures of English and German: A Contrastive Sketch.* Chicago: Univ. of Chicago Press, 1962.*

24 LADO, Robert. "A comparison of the sound systems of English and Spanish," *Hispania* 39.26-9 (1956).

25 LEHMANN, Winfred P. "Old English and Old Norse secondary preterits in -r-," *Lang* 30.202-10 (1954).

1   LEHN, Walter, and William R. SLAGER. "A contrastive study of Egyptian Arabic and American English: the segmental phonemes," *LL* 9.25-33 (1959).

2   MARCHAND, Hans. "On the question of aspect: a comparison between the progressive form in English and that in Italian and Spanish," *SL* 9.45-52 (1955).

3   MOULTON, William G. *The Sounds of English and German*. Chicago: Univ. of Chicago Press, 1962.*

4   MUELLER, Hugo. "Some German intonation patterns and their relation to stress," *MLJ* 40.28-30 (1956). [Contrast with English.]

5   SAPORTA, Sol. "Methodological considerations regarding a statistical approach to typologies," *IJAL* 23.109-13 (1957).

6   SAPORTA, Sol. "Problems in the comparison of the morphemic systems of English and Spanish," *Hispania* 39.36-40 (1956).

7   SHEN, Yao. "A grammatical contrast and its signals in Mandarin Chinese and in English," *JCLA* 6.7-13 (1960).

8   SPANG-HANSSEN, Henning. *Probability and Structural Classification in Language Description*. Copenhagen: Rosenkilde and Bagger, 1959.

9   SPITZER, Leo. "The actor-infinitive construction in Russian and other Indo-European languages," *Word* 10.442-56 (1954).

10 TRAGER, George L. "The typology of paralanguage," *AnL* 3:1.17-21 (1961).

11 VOEGELIN, Carl F., and John YEGERLEHNER. "The scope of the whole system ('distinctive feature') and subsystem typologies," *Word* 12.444-53 (1956).

12 WEINREICH, Uriel. *Languages in Contact: Findings and Problems*. New York: Linguistic Circle of New York, 1953.*

13 WEINREICH, Uriel. "On the compatibility of genetic relationship and convergent development," *Word* 14.374-79 (1958).

14 WEINREICH, Uriel. "On the description of phonic interference," *Word* 13.1-11 (1957). Also in *TESL* [71.1], 126-34.

15 ZAWADOWSKI, Leon. "Theoretical foundations of comparative grammar," *Orbis* 11.5-20 (1962).

16 ZIMMER, Karl E. *Affixal Negation in English and Other Languages: An Investigation of Restricted Productivity*. (Monograph No. 5; Supplement to *Word*, Vol. 20). New York: Linguistic Circle of New York, 1964.

Syntax

See also **88**.20 and SYNTAX, p. **54**.

17 BOLINGER, Dwight L., and Louis J. GERSTMAN. "Disjuncture as a cue to constructs," *Word* 13.246-55 (1957).

18 COLLINSON, W. E. "Some notes on the linguistic expression of composite wholes," *Lingua* 2.75-85 (1962).

19 DARNELL, Donald K. "The relation between sentence order and comprehension," *SM* 30:2.97-100 (1963).

20 DE GROOT, A. Willem. "Classification of word-groups," *Lingua* 6.113-57 (1957).

21 DE GROOT, A. Willem. "Subject-predicate analysis," *Lingua* 6.301-13 (1957).

22 DIDERICHSEN, P. "The importance of distribution versus other criteria in linguistic analysis," *P8ICL* [6.15], 156-81.

1 ELSON, Benjamin, and Velma B. PICKETT. *Beginning Morphology-Syntax.* Santa Ana, Calif.: Summer Institute of Linguistics, 1960.

2 GARVIN, Paul L. "A study of inductive method in syntax," *Word* 18.107-20 (1962).

3 HARWOOD, F. W. "Axiomatic syntax: the construction and evaluation of a syntactic calculus,"*Lang* 31.409-13 (1955).

4 LASCELLES, Monica. "A theory in distributional syntax: classes and constants," *L&S* 3.50-60 (1960).

5 LJUNGGREN, K. C. "Towards a definition of the concept of preposition," *SL* 5.7-20 (1951).

6 PARKER-RHODES, A. F. "Is there an interlingual element in syntax?" *P9ICL* [6.15], 176-90 (1964).

7 PIKE, Kenneth L. "On tagmemes, née gramemes," *IJAL* 24.273-8 (1958).*

8 PIKE, Kenneth L. "Taxemes and immediate constituents," *Lang* 19.65-82 (1943).*

9 POSTAL, Paul M. *Constituent Structure: A Study of Contemporary Models of Syntactic Description.* 's-Gravenhage: Mouton, 1964.

10 QUIRK, Randolph. "Substitutions and syntactical research," *ArL* 10.37-42 (1958).

11 SANDMANN, Manfred. *Subject and Predicate: A Contribution to the Theory of Syntax.* Edinburgh: Oliver and Boyd, 1954.

12 STAAL, J. F. "The construction of formal definitions of subject and predicate," *TPS* (1960). 89-103.

13 WILSON, Henry J. "Periodicity or structural delay," *AS* 31.25-34 (1956).

English Language and Linguistics

Backgrounds of English: Indo-European (especially Germanic)

See also 4.13.

14 ANTONSEN, Elmer H. "Germanic umlaut anew," *Lang* 37.215-30 (1961).

15 AUSTIN, William M. "Germanic reflexes of Indo-European *-hy-* and *-hw-*," *Lang* 34.203-11 (1958).

16 BENDER, Harold H. *The Home of the Indo-Europeans.* Princeton, N. J.: Princeton Univ. Press, 1932.*

17 BENNETT, William H. "The cause of the West Germanic lengthening," *Lang* 22.14-18 (1946).

18 BENNETT, William H. "The earliest Germanic umlauts and the Gothic migrations," *Lang* 28.339-42 (1952).

19 BENNETT, William H. "The Germanic development of Indo-European *ē*," *Lang* 26.232-5 (1950).

20 BENNETT, William H. "The phonemic status of Gothic *w ƕ q*," *Lang* 35.427-32 (1959).

21 BENNETT, William H. "The Southern English development of Germanic initial [f s þ]," *Lang* 31.367-71 (1955).

1 CARR, Charles T. *Nominal Compounds in Germanic*. (St. Andrews Univ. Publication no. 41.) London: Humphrey Milford, 1939.

2 COLLITZ, Hermann. "A century of Grimm's Law," *Lang* 2.174-83 (1926).*

3 DILLON, Myles. "Germanic and Celtic," *JEGP* 42.492-8 (1943).

4 EDGERTON, Franklin. "The Indo-European semivowels," *Lang* 19.83-124 (1943).

5 EDGERTON, Franklin. "The semivowel phonemes of Indo-European: a reconsideration," *Lang* 38.352-9 (1962).

6 EINARSSON, Stefán. "Terms of direction in Old Icelandic," *JEGP* 43.265-85 (1944).

7 FOWLER, Murray. "Indo-European [bh] > English /v/," *Word* 19.322-7 (1963).

8 EMENEAU, Murray B. "A note on the development of the Indo-European dental groups," *Lang* 9.232-6 (1933).

9 FEIST, Sigmund. "The origin of the Germanic languages and the Indo-Europeanizing of North Europe," *Lang* 8.245 (1932).

10 HAUGEN, Einar. *First Grammatical Treatise: The Earliest Germanic Phonology*. Language Monograph 25, supplement to *Lang* 26.4 (1950).

11 HOENIGSWALD, Henry M. "Laryngeals and *s* movable," *Lang* 28.182-5 (1952).

12 HUDSON-WILLIAMS, T. *A Short Introduction to the Study of Comparative Grammar (Indo-European)*. Cardiff: The Univ. of Wales Press Board, 1935.

13 KENT, Roland G. "The development of the Indo-European dental groups," *Lang* 8.18-26 (1932).

14 KURYŁOWICZ, Jerzy. "Morphological gemination in Keltic and Germanic," *Whatmough Studies* [6.17], 131-44.

15 KURYŁOWICZ, Jerzy. "On the methods of internal reconstruction," *P9ICL* [6.15], 9-31.

16 LANE, George S. "The genesis of the stem-vowel *u* (*o*) in the Germanic *r*-stems," *JEGP* 50.522-8 (1951).

17 LANE, George S. "On the formation of the Indo-European demonstrative," *Lang* 37.469-75 (1961).

18 LEHMANN, Winfred P. "The conservatism of Germanic phonology," *JEGP* 52.140-52 (1953).

19 LEHMANN, Winfred P. "A definition of Proto-Germanic: a study in the chronological delimitation of languages," *Lang* 37.67-74 (1961).

20 LEHMANN, Winfred P. "On earlier stages of the Indo-European nominal inflection," *Lang* 34.179-202 (1958).

21 LEHMANN, Winfred P. *Proto-Indo-European Phonology*. Austin, Tex.: Univ. of Texas, 1952.

22 LEHMANN, Winfred P. "The proto-Indo-European resonants in Germanic," *Lang* 21.355-66 (1955).

23 MAKAEV, E. A. "The morphological structure of common Germanic," *Linguistics* 10.22-50 (1964).

24 MARCHAND, James M. "The Gothic language," *Orbis* 7.492-515 (1958).

25 MARTINET, André. "Non-apophonic *o*-vocalism in Indo-European," *Word* 9.253-67 (1953).

1   MARTINET, André. "Some cases of -k-/-w- alternation in Indo-European," *Word* 12.1-6 (1956).

2   MORGENSTIERNE, Georg. "Distribution of Indo-European features surviving in modern languages," For Roman Jakobson [5.16], 367-71.

3   MOULTON, William G. "The phonemes of Gothic," *Lang* 24.76-86 (1948).

4   MOULTON, William G. "The stops and spirants of early Germanic," *Lang* 30.1-42 (1954).

5   MUST, Gustav. "Again the origin of the Germanic dental preterit," *Lang* 28.104-6 (1952).

6   MUST, Gustav. "The origin of the Germanic dental preterit," *Lang* 27.121-35 (1951).

7   PENZL, Herbert. "The development of Germanic *ai* and *au* in Old High German," *GR* 22.174-81 (1947).

8   PENZL, Herbert. "Orthography and phonemes in Wulfila's Gothic," *JEGP* 49.217-30 (1950).

9   PROKOSCH, Eduard. *A Comparative Germanic Grammar*. Philadelphia: Linguistic Society of America, 1939.*

10 PUHVEL, Jaan. "Indo-European negative composition," *Lang* 29.14-25 (1953).

11 ROBERTS, Murat H. "The antiquity of the Germanic verb-adverb locution," *JEGP* 35.466-81 (1936).

12 STRONG, Leon H., and Norman L. WILLEY. "Dynamic consonantal permutation," *JEGP* 39:1.1-12 (1940).

13 STURTEVANT, Edgar H. "The Indo-Hittite hypothesis," *Lang* 38.105-10 (1962).*

14 SWADESH, Morris. "Archaeological and linguistic chronology of Indo-European," *AA* 55.349-52 (1953).

15 SZEMERÉNYI, O. "Structuralism and substratum: Indo-Europeans and Semites in the ancient Near East," *Lingua* 13.1-29 (1964).

16 TWADDELL, W. Freeman. "A note on Old High German umlaut," *Monatshefte* 30.177-81 (1938). Also in *Readings in Linguistics* [6.6], 85-87.

17 TWADDELL, W. Freeman. "The Prehistoric German short syllabics," *Lang* 24.139-51 (1948). Also in *Readings in Linguistics* [6.6], 290-97.

18 TWADDELL, W. Freeman. "Pre-Old High German /t/," *For Roman Jakobson* [5.16], 559-66.

19 VAN COETSEM, F. "Structural linguistics and the study of Old Germanic," *Lingua* 13.30-48 (1964).

20 VELTEN, Harry V. "The order of the pre-Germanic consonant changes," *JEGP* 43.42-48 (1944).

21 WATKINS, Calvert. "Preliminaries to the reconstruction of Indo-European," *P9ICL* [6.15], 1035-42.

History of the English Language

GENERAL

See also 4.12, 73.2, 75.18, 75.20, 79.11, 79.18, 80.19, and 80.23.

22 AIKEN, Janet Rankin. *English Present and Past*. New York: Ronald Press, 1930.

1 ALEXANDER, Henry. *The Story of Our Language.* Toronto: Nelson, 1940. [Dolp C 383]

2 BAUGH, Albert C. *History of the English Language.* 2nd edition. New York: Appleton-Century-Crofts, 1957.

3 BLOOMFIELD, Morton W., and Leonard NEWMARK. *A Linguistic Introduction to the History of English.* New York: Knopf, 1963. [Reviewed by James H. Sledd in *Lang* 40.465-83 (1964).]

4 BROOK, G. L. *A History of the English Language.* London: André Deutsch, 1958. [Nort N 248]

5 BRYANT, Margaret M. *Modern English and Its Heritage.* 2nd edition. New York: Macmillan, 1962.

6 CLARK, John Williams. *Early English: A Study of Old and Middle English.* London: André Deutsch, 1957. [Nort N 228]

7 EMERSON, Oliver F. *The History of the English Language.* New York: Macmillan, 1894.

8 JACKSON, Kenneth. *Language and History in Early Britain.* Cambridge, Mass.: Harvard Univ. Press, 1954.

9 JESPERSEN, Otto. *Growth and Structure of the English Language.* 9th edition. Oxford: Basil Blackwell, 1948. [Anchor A 46] *

10 KRAPP, George Philip. *Modern English: Its Growth and Present Use.* New York: Scribner's, 1909.

11 LOUNSBURY, Thomas R. *History of the English Language.* Rev. and enlarged. New York: Holt, Rinehart and Winston, 1924.

12 MAGOUN, F. P., Jr. "Colloquial Old and Middle English," *Harvard Stud. and Notes in Philol. and Lit.* 19.167-73 (1937).

13 MARCKWARDT, Albert H. *Introduction to the English Language.* New York: Oxford Univ. Press, 1942.

14 MARSH, George P. *The Origin and History of the English Language, and of the Early Literature It Embodies,* 3rd edition. New York: Scribner, 1867.

15 McKNIGHT, George H., with the assistance of Bert Emsley. *Modern English in the Making.* New York: Appleton-Century-Crofts, 1928.

16 PYLES, Thomas. *The Origin and Development of the English Language.* New York: Harcourt, Brace and World, 1964.

17 ROBERTSON, Stuart, and Frederic G. CASSIDY. *Development of Modern English.* Rev. edition. New York: Prentice-Hall, 1954.

18 SCHLAUCH, Margaret. *The English Language in Modern Times (Since 1400).* Warsaw: Pánstwowe Wydawnictwo Naukowe, 1959. (In America, Oxford Univ. Press.)

19 TUCKER, Susie I. *English Examined: Two Centuries of Comment on the Mother Tongue.* Cambridge: Cambridge Univ. Press, 1961.

20 WRENN, C. L. *The English Language.* London: Methuen, 1949.

21 WYLD, Henry Cecil. *The Historical Study of the Mother Tongue. An Introduction to Philological Method.* London: Murray, 1907.

22 WYLD, Henry Cecil. *A History of Modern Colloquial English.* Rev. ed. New York: Peter Smith, 1936.

23 WYLD, Henry Cecil. *A Short History of English.* 3rd edition, rev. and enlarged. London: Murray, 1927.

HISTORICAL GRAMMAR

1 BAZELL, C. E. "Six questions of Old and Middle English morphology," *Tolkien Studies* [5.9], 51-62.

2 BLOOMFIELD, Morton W., and Benjamin A. EILBOTT. "A diachronic approach to lexical number: Middle and Modern English," *AS* 32.170-75 (1957).

3 BØGHOLM, N. *English Speech from an Historical Point of View.* Copenhagen: Nyt Nordisk Forlag; London: Allen and Unwin, 1939.

4 CALLAWAY, Morgan, Jr. "Concerning the origin of the gerund in English," *Klaeber Miscellany* [6.10], 32-49.

5 COLLINGE, N. E. "Some reflexions on comparative historical syntax," *ArL* 12.79-101 (1960).

6 EINARSSON, Stefán. "Functional change in early English," *MLN* 64.498-500 (1949).

7 ELLEGÅRD, Alvar. *The Auxiliary do: The Establishment and Regulation of Its Use in English.* (*GothSE*, vol. 2). Stockholm: Almqvist & Wiksell, 1953.

8 FRAENKEL, Gerd. "The decline of Latin as a model for linguistic analysis," *P9ICL* [6.15], 730-37.

9 FRIDÉN, George. "On the use of auxiliaries to form the perfect and the pluperfect in late Middle English and Early Modern English," *Archiv* 196.152-3 (1959).

10 FRIDÉN, George. *Studies on the Tenses of the English Verb from Chaucer to Shakespeare, with Special Reference to the Late Sixteenth Century.* (Essays and Studies on English Lang. and Lit., vol. 2). Uppsala and Cambridge: Harvard Univ. Press, 1948.

11 FRIES, Charles C. "On the development of the structural use of word-order in Modern English," *Lang* 16.199-208 (1940).

12 HARTUNG, Charles V. "The persistence of tradition in grammar," *QJS* 48.174-186 (1962).

13 HELTVIET, Trygve. *Studies in English Demonstrative Pronouns: A Contribution to the History of English Morphology.* Oslo: Akademisk Forlag, 1953.

14 KARLBERG, Göran. *The English Interrogative Pronouns: A Study of Their Syntactic History.* GothSE, No. 3, Stockholm: Almqvist & Wiksell, 1954.

15 KELLNER, Leon, *Historical Outlines of English Syntax.* London: Macmillan, 1892 (repr. 1924).

16 LEE, Donald W. *Functional Change in Early English.* Menasha, Wis.: Banta, 1949. (Columbia Univ. diss.).

17 LEHNERT, Martin. "The interrelation between form and function in the development of the English language," *ZAA* 5.43-56 (1957).

18 LEVIN, Samuel R. "Negative contraction: an old and middle English dialect criterion," *JEGP* 57.492-501 (1958).

19 MÄTZNER, Eduard. *An English Grammar; Methodical, Analytical, and Historical,* 3 vols., 3d edition, Tr. by Clair James Grece. London, J. Murray, 1880-85.*

1   MARCHAND, Hans. "The syntactical change from inflectional to word order system and some effects of this change on the relation 'verb/object' in English: A diachronic-synchronic interpretation," *Anglia* 70:1.70-89 (1951).

2   MEECH, Sanford B. "Early application of Latin grammar to English," *PMLA* 50.1012-31 (1935).

3   MOORE, Samuel. *Historical Outlines of English Sounds and Inflections*, revised by Albert H. Marckwardt. Ann Arbor, Mich.: Wahr, 1957.*

4   Ross, Alan S. C. "The origin of the s-endings of the present indicative in English," *JEGP* 33.68-73 (1934).

5   STOCKWELL, Robert P. "On the utility of an over-all pattern in historical English phonology," *P9ICL* [6.15], 663-69.

6   TRNKA, B. "On the phonological development of spirants in English," *P2ICPS* [6.16], 60-64.

7   TRNKA, B. "A phonemic aspect of the Great Vowel Shift," *Mélanges Fernand Mossé* [6.12], 440-43.

8   VACHEK, Josef. "Notes on the quantitative correlation of vowels in the phonematic development of English." *Mélanges Fernand Mossé* [6.12], 444-56.

9   VICKERS, Wallace J. "A historical study of the concept of case in English grammar," *Stanford Univ. Abstracts of Dissertations* 1.102-5 (1927).

OLD ENGLISH

See also 3.11, 3.21, and 4.11.

10   ANDERSON, George K. "The fifth case in Old English," *JEGP* 57.21-6 (1958).

11   ANDREW, S. O. "Relative and demonstrative pronouns in Old English," *Lang* 12.282-93 (1936).

12   ANDREW, S. O. *Syntax and Style in Old English*. Cambridge: Cambridge Univ. Press; New York: Macmillan, 1940.

13   BARRETT, C. R. *Studies in the Word-Order of Ælfric's Catholic Homilies and Lives of the Saints*. Cambridge: Cambridge Univ. Press, 1953.

14   BAUER, Gerd. "The problem of short diphthongs in Old English," *Anglia* 74.427-37 (1956).

15   BAZELL, C. E. "Some problems of Old English morphology," *Mélanges Fernand Mossé* [6.12], 27-31.

16   BLAKELEY, L. "Accusative-dative syncretism in the Lindisfarne Gospels," *Eng. and Germanic Studies* (Univ. of Birmingham) 1.6-31 (1947-48).

17   BLOOMFIELD, Leonard. "Notes on the preverb *ge-* in Alfredian English," *Klaeber Miscellany* [6.10], 79-102.

18   BROOK, G. L. *An Introduction to Old English*. Manchester: Univ. Press, 1955.

19   BROSNAHAN, L. F. *Some Old English Sound Changes: An Analysis.in the Light of Modern Phonetics*. Cambridge: Heffer, 1953.

20   BRUNNER, Karl. "The Old English vowel phonemes," *ES* 34.247-51 (1953).

21   CALLAWAY, Morgan, Jr. *The Consecutive Subjunctive in Old English*. (Modern Lang. Assoc. of America Monograph Series, No. 4). Boston: Heath, 1933.*

22   CAMPBELL, Alistair. *Old English Grammar*. Oxford: Clarendon Press, 1959.*

1 CARLTON, Charles. "Word order of noun modifiers in Old English prose," *JEGP* 62.778-83 (1963).

2 CHATMAN, Seymour. "The a/æ opposition in Old English," *Word.* 14.224-36 (1958).

3 DAHL, Ivar. *Substantive Inflexion in Early Old English, Vocalic Stems.* LSE 7. Lund: Gleerup, 1938.

4 DAUNT, Marjorie. "Old English sound-changes reconsidered in relation to scribal tradition and practice," *TPS* 1939, 108-38.

5 DECAMP, David. "The genesis of the Old English dialects: a new hypothesis," *Lang* 34.232-44 (1958).

6 DEROLEZ, René. "Norm and practice in late Old English," *P8ICL* [**6.15**], 18.415-17.

7 ELIASON, Norman E. "Old English vowel lengthening and vowel shortening before consonant groups," *SP* 45.1-20 (1948).

8 ELLIOTT, Ralph W. V. *Runes: An Introduction.* Manchester: Univ. Press, 1959.

9 FUNKE, Otto. "Some remarks on late Old English word-order with special reference to Ælfric and the Maldon poem [about 991]," *ES* 37.99-104 (1956).

10 GRADON, Pamela. "Studies in late West-Saxon labialization and delabialization," *Tolkien Studies* [**5.9**], 63-76.

11 GREENFIELD, Stanley B. "Syntactic analysis and Old English poetry," *NM* 64.373-8 (1963).

12 HALLQVIST, Henning. *Studies in Old English Fractured ea.* LSE, Vol. 14. Lund: Gleerup, 1948.

13 HEDBERG, Johannes. *The Syncope of the Old English Present Endings.* LSE. Lund: C. W. K. Gleerup, 1945.

14 HOCKETT, Charles F. "The stressed syllabics of Old English," *Lang* 35.575-97 (1959).

15 KUHN, Sherman M. "On the syllabic phonemes of Old English," *Lang* 37.522-38 (1961).

16 KUHN, Sherman M., and Randolph QUIRK. "Some recent interpretations of the Old English digraph spellings," *Lang* 29.143-56 (1953).

17 LEHMANN, Winfred P. "Metrical evidence for Old English suprasegmentals," *TSLL* 1.66-72 (1959).

18 LEVIN, Samuel R. "A reclassification of the Old English strong verbs," *Lang* 40.156-61 (1964).

19 LINDEMANN, J. W. Richard. "Old English preverbal *ge-*: a re-examination of some current doctrines," *JEGP* 64.65-83 (1965).

20 LÖFVENBERG, Mattias T. *On the Syncope of the Old English Present Endings.* Uppsala: Lundquist, 1949.

21 MARCKWARDT, Albert H., ed. *Laurence Nowell's* Vocabularium Saxonicum. Ann Arbor: Univ. of Michigan Press, 1952.

22 MARCKWARDT, Albert H. "Origin and extension of the voiceless preterit and the past participle inflections of the English irregular weak verb conjunction," *Essays and Studies by Members of the Eng. Dept. of the Univ. of Mich.* Ann Arbor: Univ. of Michigan Press, 1935, 151-328.

23 MARCKWARDT, Albert H. "Verb inflections in late Old English," *Philologica* [**6.8**], 79-88.

1 MARCKWARDT, Albert H. "The verbal suffix *-ettan* in Old English," *Lang* 18.275-81 (1942).

2 MERITT, Herbert Dean. *Fact and Lore about Old English Words*. Palo Alto, Calif.: Stanford Univ. Press, 1954.

3 MITCHELL, Bruce. "Pronouns in Old English poetry: some syntactical notes," *RES*, N. S. 15.129-41 (1964).

4 MOORE, Samuel, and Thomas A. KNOTT. *The Elements of Old English*, 8th edition, rev. and enlarged. Ann Arbor, Mich.: Wahr, 1940.

5 NIST, John A. "Phonemics and distinctive features of *Beowulf*," *SIL* 13.25-33 (1958).

6 PELTOLA, Niilo. "On appositional constructions in Old English prose," *NM* 61.159-203 (1960).

7 PENZL, Herbert. "A phonemic change in early Old English," *Lang* 20.84-7 (1944).

8 PENZL, Herbert. "The phonemic split of Germanic *k* in Old English," *Lang* 23.34-42 (1947).

9 POPE, J. C. *The Rhythm of Beowulf*. New Haven: Yale Univ. Press, 1949.

10 PROKOSCH, Eduard. "The Old English weak preterites without medial vowel," *PMLA* 42.331-8 (1927).

11 PYLES, Thomas. "The pronunciation of Latin learned loan words and foreign words in Old English," *PMLA* 58.891-910 (1943).

12 QUIRK, Randolph. *The Concessive Relation in Old English Poetry*. New Haven: Yale Univ. Press, 1954.

13 QUIRK, Randolph. "On the problem of morphological suture in Old English," *MLR* 45.1-5 (1950).

14 QUIRK, Randolph, and C. L. WRENN. *An Old English Grammar*, 2nd edition. London: Methuen, 1958.

15 ROSS, Alan S. C. "Old English æ ~ a," *ES* 32.50-56 (1951).

16 SAMUELS, M. L. "The study of Old English phonology," *TPS* 1952, 15-28.

17 SCHERER, Philip. "Aspect in the Old English of the Corpus Christi MS," *Lang* 34.245-51 (1958).

18 SHANNON, Ann. *A Descriptive Syntax of the Parker Manuscript of the Anglo-Saxon Chronicle from 734 to 891 (Janua Linguarum,* series Practica, 14). 's-Gravenhage: Mouton, 1964.

19 SLETTERGREN, Emrik. "On the development of OE initial *sc*," *SiMS* 15.45-50 (1943).

20 SMALL, G. W. "On the study of Old English syntax," *PMLA* 51.1-7 (1936).

21 STANLEY, E. G. "The chronology of r-metathesis in Old English," *English and Germanic Studies* 5.103-15 (1952-53).

22 STERN, Gustav. "On methods of interpretation," *SN* 17.35-41 (1944).

23 STOCKWELL, Robert P. "The phonology of Old English: a structural sketch," *SIL* 13.13-24 (1958).

24 STOCKWELL, Robert P., and C. Westbrook BARRITT. "The Old English short digraphs: some considerations," *Lang* 31.372-89. Reply by Sherman M. Kuhn and Randolph Quirk, 390-401 (1955).

25 STOCKWELL, Robert P., and C. Westbrook BARRITT. *Some Old English Graphemic-phonemic Correspondences — æ, ea, and a. (SILOP,* No. 4). Washington: Studies in Linguistics, 1951.

1 TENGVIK, Gösta. *Old English Bynames*. Uppsala: Almqvist and Wiksell, 1938.

2 WALKER, James A. "The rank-number relationship of adjectival suffixes in Old English," *PQ* 27.264-72 (1948).

3 WEMAN, Bertil. *Old English Semantic Analysis and Theory with Special Reference to Verbs Denoting Locomotion*. LSE, E. Ekwall, ed. Lund: Lindstedt, 1933.

4 WRIGHT, Joseph and Elizabeth M. *Old English Grammar*, 3d edition. London: Oxford Univ. Press, 1925.

MIDDLE ENGLISH

See also **3**.3, **3**.17, **76**.22, and **85**.6.

5 ACKERMAN, Robert W. *An Index of the Arthurian Names in Middle English*. Stanford: Stanford Univ. Publications in Language and Literature, Vol. 10. (1952).

6 BENSON, L. D. "Chaucer's historical present. Its meaning and uses," *ES* 42.65-77 (1961).

7 BØGHOLM, N. *The Layamon Texts: A Linguistical Investigation*. Copenhagen: Munksgaard, 1944.

8 BOHMAN, Hjördis. *Studies in the Midde English dialects of Devon and London*. Göteborg: Pehrsson, 1944.

9 BRUNNER, Karl. *An Outline of Middle English Grammar*, tr. by Grahame Johnston. Cambridge: Harvard Univ. Press, 1963.

10 BURCHFIELD, R. W. "The language and orthography of the Ormulum MS," *TPS* 1956, 56-87 (1957).

11 CONNER, J. E. "Phonemic discrimination of Middle English dialects," *Rice Institute Pamphlet*, 44.18-32 (1957).

12 DEAN, Christopher. "Chaucer's use of function words with substantives," *CJL* 9.67-74 (1964).

13 DICKINS, Bruce, and R. M. WILSON. "Characteristics of Early Middle English," in *Early Middle English Texts*, ed. Bruce Dickins and R. M. Wilson. New York: W. W. Norton, 1951.

14 DOBSON, Eric John. "Middle English lengthening in open syllables," *TPS, 1962*, 124-48 (1963).

15 DONALDSON, E. Talbot. "Chaucer's final -*e*," *PMLA* 63.1101-24 (1948).

16 ENGBLOM, Victor. *On the Origin and Early Development of the Auxiliary 'Do.'* (LSE, 6). Lund: C. W. K. Gleerup, 1938.

17 FORSTRÖM, Gösta. *The Verb "to be" in Middle English: a Survey of the Forms*. (*LSE* vol. 15). Lund: Gleerup, 1948.

18 HARRIS, David Payne. "The development of word-order patterns in twelfth-century English," *Fries Studies* [**6**.11], 187-98.

19 HULBERT, J. R. "English in manorial documents of the thirteenth and fourteenth centuries," *MP* 34.37-61 (1936).

20 KOBAYASHI, Eichi. "The Verb Forms of the 'South English Legendary'," (*Janua Linguarum*, Series Practica, 15). 's-Gravenhage: Mouton, 1964.

21 KÖKERITZ, Helge. "English *i* for Old French *ü*," *Mélanges Fernand Mossé* [**6**.12], 218-24.

22 KURATH, Hans. "The loss of long consonants and the rise of voiced fricatives in Middle English," *Lang* 32.435-45 (1956).

1 LANGENFELT, Gösta. *Select Studies in Colloquial English of the Late Middle Ages.* Lund: Gleerup, 1933.

2 LONG, Mary M. *The English Strong Verb from Chaucer to Caxton.* Menasha, Wis.: Banta, 1944.

3 MALONE, Kemp. "When did Middle English begin?" *Curme Studies* [5.17], 110-17.

4 McINTOSH, Angus. "The analysis of written Middle English," *TPS*, 1956, 26-55 (1957).

5 McINTOSH, Angus. "A new approach to Middle English dialectology." *ES* 44.1-11 (1963).

6 McJIMSEY, Ruth B. *"Chaucer's Irregular -e: A Demonstration among Monosyllabic Nouns of the Exceptions to Grammatical and Metrical Harmony.* New York: King's Crown Press, 1942.

7 MERONEY, Howard. "The early history of *down* as an adverb." *JEGP* 44.378-86 (1945).

8 MOORE, Samuel. "Earliest morphological changes in Middle English," *Lang* 4.238-66 (1928).

9 MOORE, Samuel. "Loss of final *n* in inflectional syllables of Middle English," *Lang* 3.232-59 (1927).

10 MOSSÉ, Fernand. *A Handbook of Middle English,* trans. James A. Walker. Baltimore: The Johns Hopkins Press, 1952.

11 MUSTANOJA, Tauno F. *A Middle English Syntax,* Pt. 1: Parts of Speech. Helsinki: Société Néophilologique, 1960.

12 NATHAN, Norman. "Pronouns of address in the *Canterbury Tales.*" *MS* 21.193-201 (1959).

13 OHLANDER, Urban. *Studies on Coordinate Expressions in Middle English.* (LSE vol. 5). Lund: Gleerup, 1936.

14 OHLANDER, Urban. "A study on the use of the infinitive sign in Middle English," *SN* 14.58-66 (1941-2).

15 ORTON, Harold. "The isolative treatment in living North-Midland dialects of OE e lengthened in open syllables in Middle English," *Leeds Studies in English and Kindred Languages* 7-8.97-128 (1952).

16 PRINS, A. A. "On the loss and substitution of words in Middle English," *Neophil* 26.280-98; 27.49-59 (1941-42).

17 RANTAVAARA, Irma. "On the development of the periphrastic dative in late Middle English prose," *NM* 63.175-203 (1962).

18 REED, David W. "The history of inflectional *n* in English verbs before 1500," *Univ. of Calif. Pbns. in English* 7:4.157-328 (1950).

19 RESZKIEWICZ, Alred. *Main Sentence Elements in* The Book of Margery Kempe. Warsaw: Polish Academy of Sciences, 1962.

20 RETTGER, J. F. *The Development of Ablaut in the Strong Verbs of the East Midland Dialects of Middle English.* (Language Dissertations) Philadelphia: Ling. Soc. of America, vol. 18, 1934.

21 ROSEBOROUGH, Margaret M. *An Outline of Middle English Grammar.* New York: Macmillan, 1938.

22 SAMUELS, M. L. "Some applications of Middle English dialectology," *ES* 44.81-94 (1963).

23 SISAM, Kenneth. "The English language in the fourteenth century," appendix to *Fourteenth Century Verse and Prose,* ed. Kenneth Sisam. Oxford: Clarendon Press, 1925.

1 SOUTHWORTH, James G. "Chaucer's final *-e* in rhyme," *PMLA* 62.910-35 (1947); (continued) *PMLA* 64.601-9 (1949).

2 STEVICK, Robert D. "Plus juncture and the spelling of the *Ormulum*," *JEGP* 64.84-9 (1964).

3 STOBIE, Margaret M. R. "The influence of morphology on Middle English alliterative poetry," *JEGP* 39.319-36 (1940).

4 STOCKWELL, Robert P. "The Middle English 'long close' and 'long open' vowels," *TSLL* 2. 529-38 (1960).

5 SWIECZKOWSKI, Walerian. *Word Order Patterning in Middle English: a quantitative study based on* Piers Plowman *and Middle English Sermons.* (*Janua Linguarum,* Series Minor, No. 19.) 's-Gravenhage: Mouton, 1962.

6 WARDALE, Edith E. *An Introduction to Middle English.* London: Kegan Paul, Trench, Trubner, 1937.

7 WHITING, Bartlett Jere. "The rime of King William," *Philologica* [6.8], 89-96.

8 WILSON, R. M. "English and French in England, 1100-1300," *History* 28.37-60 (1943).

9 WOODBINE, G. E. "The language of English law," *Speculum* 18.395-486 (1943).

10 WRIGHT, Joseph and Elizabeth M. *An Elementary Middle English Grammar.* London: Oxford Univ. Press, 1932.

11 WYLD, Henry Cecil. "Studies in the diction of Layamon's *Brut*," *Lang* 9.47-71 (1933). Pt. II. *Lang* 13.194-237 (1937).

EARLY MODERN ENGLISH

See also **85**.15 and **86**.2.

12 ABBOTT, Edwin A. *A Shakespearian Grammar.* New edition. London: Macmillan, 1888.

13 ABBOTT, O. L. "The formal subjunctive in seventeenth-century American English," *AS* 36.181-7 (1961).

14 ABBOTT, O. L. "The preterit and past participles of strong verbs in seventeenth-century American English," *AS* 32.31-42 (1957).

15 ABBOTT, O. L. "Verbal endings in seventeenth-century American English," *AS* 33.185-94 (1958).

16 BAMBAS, Rudolph C. "Verb forms in -s and -th in Early Modern English," *JEGP* 46.183-7 (1947).

17 BERGSTRØM, Folke. "John Kirkby (1746) on English pronunciation," *SN* 27.65-104 (1955).

18 BREWSTER, Paul G. "A note on the 'Winchester goose' and kindred topics," *Journal of the History of Medicine and Allied Sciences* 13.483-91 (1958).

19 BRONSTEIN, Arthur J., and Esther K. SHELDON. "Derivatives of Middle English ō in eighteenth- and nineteenth-century dictionaries," *AS* 26.81-9 (1951).

20 BRUNNER, Karl. "Expanded verbal forms in Early Modern English," *ES* 36.218-21 (1955).

21 BYRNE, Sister St. Geraldine. *Shakespeare's Use of the Pronoun of Address; its Significance in Characterization and Motivation.* Washington, D. C.: Catholic Univ. of America Ph. D. Dissertation 36.

1 DAHL, Torsten. *Linguistic Studies in Some Elizabethan Writings.* Vol. II: *The Auxiliary* Do. (Acta Jutlandica, Univ. of Aarhus Pubns. vol. 28, pt. 2; Humanities Series 42). Copenhagen: Munksgaard; New York: G. Lounz, 1956.

2 DAVIES, Constance. *English Pronounciation from the Fifteenth to the Eighteenth Century.* London: Dent, 1934.

3 DOBBIE, Elliott V. K. "On Early Modern English pronunciation," *AS* 33.111-15 (1958). [Review of E. J. Dobson. See **48**.5.]

4 DOBSON, Eric John. "Early Modern standard English," *TPS* 1955.25-54 (1956).

5 DOBSON, Eric John. *English Pronunciation, 1500-1700,* 2 vols. Oxford: Clarendon Press, 1957.*

6 EMMA, Ronald David. *Milton's Grammar (Studies in English Literature,* II). 's-Gravenhage: Mouton, 1964.

7 HULME, Hilda M. *Explorations in Shakespeare's Language: Some Problems of Lexical Meaning in the Dramatic Text.* London: Longmans, 1962.

8 HULTZÉN, Lee S. "Seventeenth century intonation," *AS* 14:1.39-43 (1939).

9 JOHNSON, F. R. "Latin versus English: the sixteenth-century debate over scientific terminology," *SP* 41.109-35 (1944).

10 JONES, Richard F. "Science and language in England of the mid-seventeenth century," *JEGP* 31.315-31 (1932).

11 KÖKERITZ, Helge. "English pronunciation as described in shorthand systems of the seventeenth and eighteenth centuries," *SN* 7.73-146 (1935).

12 KÖKERITZ, Helge. "Guy Miège's pronunciation (1685)," *Lang* 19.141-6 (1943).

13 KÖKERITZ, Helge. *Shakespeare's Pronunciation.* New Haven: Yale Univ. Press, 1953.*

14 MATTHEWS, William. "English pronunciation and shorthand in the Early Modern period," *Univ. of Calif. Pubs. in English* 9:3.135-214 (1943).*

15 MATTHEWS, William. Two notes on seventeenth century pronunciation," *JEGP* 32.296-300 (1933).

16 MATTHEWS, William. "Variant pronunciations in the seventeenth century," *JEGP* 37.189-206 (1938).

17 PRICE, Hereward T. "Grammar and the compositor in the sixteenth and seventeenth centuries," *JEGP* 38.540-48 (1939).

18 ROBINSON, J. W. "The composition of the Towneley Talents Play: a linguistic examination," *JEGP* 58.423-33 (1959).

19 SALMON, Vivian. "Early seventeenth-century pronunciation as a guide to sentence structure," *RES,* n.s., 13.347-60 (1962).

20 SCHOLL, Evelyn H. "New light on seventeenth century pronunciation from the English school of lutenist song writers," *PMLA* 59.398-445 (1944).

21 SHELDON, Esther K. "Walker's influence on the pronunciation of English," *PMLA* 62.130-47 (1947).

22 SUGDEN, Herbert W. *The Grammar of Spenser's Faerie Queene.* Lang. Diss. 32, Supplement to *Lang,* 1936.

23 WHITEHALL, Harold. *Middle English ū and Related Sounds, Their Development in Early American English. Lang,* Monograph 19. Baltimore: Linguistic Society of America, 15:4, 1939.

24 WHITEHALL, Harold. "The quality of the front reduction vowel in Early American English," *AS* 15.136-43 (1940).

1 WHITEHALL, Harold, and Theresa FEIN. "The development of Middle English *ŭ* in Early Modern British and American English." *JEGP* 40.191-213 (1941).

2 WRIGHT, Joseph and Elizabeth M. *An Elementary Historical New English Grammar*. London: Oxford Univ. Press, 1924.

Present-day English Grammar

GENERAL

See also **70**.10, **84**.7, and **87**.18.

3 FRANCIS, W. Nelson. *The Structure of American English*. New York: Ronald Press, 1958.

4 FRIES, Charles C. *American English Grammar*, National Council of Teachers of English Monograph No. 10. New York: Appleton-Century-Crofts, 1940.*

5 GLEASON, H. A., Jr. *Linguistics and English Grammar*. New York: Holt, Rinehart and Winston, 1965.

6 JESPERSEN, Otto. *Essentials of English Grammar*. New York: Holt, Rinehart and Winston, 1933; repr. University, Ala.: Univ. of Alabama Press, 1964.

7 JESPERSEN, Otto. *A Modern English Grammar on Historical Principles*, 7 vols. Copenhagen: Einer Munksgaard, 1909–1949; repr. London: Allen and Unwin, 1954.*

8 JOOS, Martin. *The English Verb: Form and Meaning*. Madison, Wis.: Univ. of Wisconsin Press, 1964.*

9 JUILLAND, Alphonse G., and James MACRIS. *The English Verb System*. (*Janua Linguarum* 24). 's-Gravenhage: Mouton, 1962.

10 KENNEDY, Arthur G. *Current English*. Boston: Ginn and Co., 1935.

11 KRAPP, George Philip. *The Knowledge of English*. New York: Holt, Rinehart and Winston, 1927.

12 KRUISINGA, Etsko. *A Handbook of Present-Day English*, 5th edition, 3 vols. Groningen: P. Noordhoff, 1931.*

13 PALMER, Harold E., and F. G. BLANDFORD. *Grammar of Spoken English on a Strictly Phonetic Basis*. Revised ed. Cambridge, Eng.: Heffer & Sons, 1939.

14 POUTSMA, H. *A Grammar of Late Modern English*. Groningen: P. Nordhof, Part 1, 2nd edition, 1928–1929; Part 2, 1926.*

15 QUIRK, Randolph. *The Use of English*. London, Longmans, Green, 1962.

16 ROBERTS, Paul. *Understanding Grammar*. New York: Harper and Row, 1954.

17 SLEDD, James H. *A Short Introduction to English Grammar*. Chicago: Scott, Foresman and Co., 1959.

18 SMITH, Logan Pearsall. *The English Language*. 2nd edition. New York: Oxford, 1954.

19 SONNENSCHEIN, E. A. *The Soul of Grammar*. Cambridge: Cambridge Univ. Press, 1927.

20 STRANG, Barbara M. H. *Modern English Structure*. London: E. Arnold, 1962.

21 SWEET, Henry. *A New English Grammar, Logical and Historical*. Oxford: Clarendon Press, 1891–98.

1 TRAGER, George L., and Henry Lee SMITH, Jr. *An Outline of English Structure. SIL:* Occasional Papers, 3. Norman, Okla., 1951. Repr. Washington: American Council of Learned Societies, 1963. [Review by James Sledd, *Lang* 31.312-35 (1955).]*

2 WHITEHALL, Harold. *Structural Essentials of English.* New York: Harcourt, Brace and World, 1956.

3 ZANDVOORT, R. W. "Grammatical terminology," *English Studies Today* 11.283-94 (1961).

4 ZANDVOORT, R. W. *A Handbook of English Grammar.* Rev. London: Longmans, Green, 1961.*

MORPHEMICS

See also **2**.7, **67**.5, **74**.14, **75**.4, **79**.20, **86**.9, and *Computational and Mathematical . . . ,* p. **9**, *Phonemics,* p. **20**, and *Compounds,* p. **75**.

5 BERKELEY, David S. "Agreement of subject and verb in anticipatory *there* clauses," *AS* 28.92-96 (1953).

6 BLAKE, Frank R. "A semantic analysis of case," *Lang. Monograph,* no. 7, Philadelphia: Ling. Soc. of America, 1930. Also in *Curme Studies* [5.17], 34-49.

7 BLOCH, Bernard. "English verb inflection," *Lang* 23.399-418 (1947).

8 BOLINGER, Dwight L. "More on the present tense in English," *Lang* 23.434-6 (1947).

9 BRAAKSMA, M. H. "Has modern English a genitive plural?" *ES* 23.65-74 (1941).

10 BRYAN, W. F. "The preterite and the perfect tense in present-day English," *JEGP* 35.363-82 (1936).

11 BRYANT, Margaret M. *A Functional English Grammar.* Boston: D. C. Heath, 1950.

12 CALLAWAY, Morgan, Jr. "The number of cases in modern English," *PMLA* 42.238-54 (1927).

13 CALVER, Edward. "The use of the present tense forms in English," *Lang* 22.317-25 (1946).

14 CASSIDY, Frederic G. " 'Case' in modern English," *Lang* 13.240-45 (1937).

15 CHARLESTON, Britta M. "A reconsideration of the problem of time, tense, and aspect in modern English," *ES* 36.263-78 (1955).

16 COLLINSON, W. E. "The soul of grammar and the philosophy of grammar with special reference to the question of English cases," *MLR* 23.129-44 (1928).

17 CURME, George O. *Parts of Speech and Accidence.* Boston: D. C. Heath, 1935.*

18 DOODKORTE, A. C. J., and R. W. ZANDVOORT. "On the stressing of prepositions," *ES* 43.96-101 (1962).

19 FRIES, Charles C. "Some notes on the inflected genitive in present-day English," *Lang* 14.121-33 (1938).

20 GLEITMAN, Lila R. "Pronominals and stress in English conjunctions," *LL* 11.157-69 (1961).

21 HARWOOD, F. W., and Alison M. WRIGHT. "Statistical study of English word formation," *Lang* 32.260-73 (1956).

22 HIRTLE, W. H. "The English present subjunctive," *CJL* 9.75-82 (1964).

1 HORNBY, A. S. "Non-conclusive verbs," *Eng. Lang. Tchg.* 3.172-8 (1949).

2 KENYON, John S. "One of those who is . . ," *AS* 26.161-5 (1951).

3 KINGDON, Roger. "A new table on the anomalous finites," *Eng. Lang. Tchg.* 3.206-16 (1949).

4 LAMBERTS, J. J. "How dead is congruence?" *Fries Studies* [**6**.11], 213-27.

5 LANGENFELT, Gösta. "The roots of the propword *one,*" *SiMS* 16.97-138 (1946).

6 LASCELLES, Monica. "Fries on word classes." *L&S* 2.86-105 (1959).

7 LINDKVIST, Karl-Gunnar. *Studies on the Local Sense of the Prepositions* in, at, on, *and* to *in Modern English.* (*LSE* vol. 20). Lund: Gleerup, 1950.

8 MARCHAND, Hans. "The negative verbal prefixes in English," *Mélanges Fernand Mossé* [**6**.12], 267-76.

9 MARCHAND, Hans. "Notes on English suffixation," *NM* 54.246-72 (1953).

10 RORERTS, Paul. "Fries's Group D," *Lang* 31.20-24 (1955).

11 ROBINS, R. H. "In defence of WP," *TPS* 1959, 116-44.

12 ROSS, Alan S. C. "Linguistic class indicators in present-day English," *NM* 55.20-56 (1954).

13 SØRENSEN, Holger Steen. *Word-Classes in Modern English.* Copenhagen: G. E. C. Gad, 1958.

14 SPITZBARDT, Harry. "On the grammatical categories of present participle and gerund in English," *ZAA* 6.29-45 (1958).

15 TRNKA, B. "Analysis and synthesis in English," *ES* 10.138-44 (1928).

16 TRNKA, B. "On the morphological classification of words," *Lingua* 11.422-5 (1962).

17 TROTTER, Philip. "Inchoative verbs," *Eng. Lang. Tchg.* 3.95-105 (1949).

18 VANNECK, Gerard. "The colloquial preterite in modern American English," *Word* 14.237-42 (1958).

19 ZANDVOORT, R. W. "On the so-called subjunctive," *Eng. Lang. Tchg.* 17.73-7 (1963).

PHONEMICS

See also **24**.12, **25**.3, **25**.5, **25**.13, **25**.21, **26**.9, **74**.12, **75**.9, **83**.2, **85**.9-10, **85**.19, **85**.21, **86**.11, **87**.4, and *Phonemics*, p. **20**.

20 BLOOMFIELD, Leonard. "The stressed vowels of American English," *Lang* 11.97-116 (1935).*

21 CAFFEE, Nathaniel M. "The phonemic structure of unstressed vowels in English," *AS* 26.103-9 (1951).

22 CHOMSKY, Noam, Morris HALLE, and Fred LUKOFF. "On accent and juncture in English," *For Roman Jakobson* [**5**.16], 65-80.

23 COHEN, A. *The Phomenes of English: A Phonemic Study of the Vowels and Consonants of Standard English.* s'Gravenhage: Nijhoff, 1952.

24 FISCHER-JØRGENSEN, Eli. "Kenneth L. Pike's analysis of American English intonation," *Lingua* 2.3-13 (1949).

25 HAYDEN, Rebecca E. "The relative frequency of phonemes in General-American English," *Word* 6.217-23 (1950).

26 HOLMBERG, Börje. "Notes on the modern English development of ME $\check{u}$ in stressed position compared with the neutral vowel /ə/," *SL* 11.47-53 (1958).

1 HULTZÉN, Lee S. "System status of obscured vowels in English," *Lang* 37.565-9 (1961).

2 HULTZÉN, Lee S., Joseph H. D. ALLEN, Jr., and Murray S. MIRON. *Tables of Transitional Frequencies of English Phonemes.* Urbana, Ill.: Univ. of Illinois Press, 1964.

3 JASSEM, Wiktor. *Intonation of Conversational English (Educated Southern British).* Warsaw: Nakladem Wroclawskiego Towarzystwa Naukowego, 1952.

4 KING, Harold V. "English internal juncture and syllable division," *Fries Studies* [6.11], 199-211.

5 LEE, W. R. "English intonation: a new approach," *Lingua* 5.345-71 (1956).

6 NORDHJEM, Bent. *The Phonemes of English: An Experiment in Structural Phonemics.* Copenhagen: Gad, 1960.

7 PIERCE, Joe E. "Phonemic theory and the analysis of English syllabic nuclei," *Linguistics* 7.63-82 (1964).

8 PIKE, Kenneth L. "On the phonemic status of English diphthongs," *Lang* 23.151-9 (1947).*

9 SHARF, Donald J. "Distinctiveness of 'voiced T' words," *AS* 35.105-9 (1960).

10 SHARP, A. E. "The analysis of stress and juncture in English," *TPS* 105-35 (1960).

11 SIGURD, Bengt. "English diphthongs from a structural point of view," *SL* 10.67-76 (1956).

12 SWADESH, Morris. "On the analysis of English syllabics," *Lang* 23.137-50 (1947).

13 TRAGER, George L., and Bernard BLOCH. "The syllabic phonemes of English," *Lang* 17.223-46 (1941).*

14 TRNKA, B. *A Phonological Analysis of Present-day Standard English.* Prague: Studies in English by Members of the English Seminar of the Charles Univ., Vol. 5, 1935.

15 VACHEK, Josef. "The phonematic status of modern English long vowels and diphthongs," *PP* 6:1.59-71 (1963).

16 WANG, William S. Y. "Stress in English," *LL* 12.69-77 (1962).

17 WELLS, Rulon S. "The pitch phonemes of English," *Lang* 21.27-39 (1945).*

PHONETICS

See also **1**.18, **3**.9, **3**.15-16, **26**.9, **26**.21, **74**.19, **79**.11, **79**.18, **80**.6, **80**.18, and *Phonetics*/GENERAL, p. **22**.

18 ABEL, James W. "Syllabic [m,ŋ]," *AS* 37.106-13 (1962).

19 ABEL, James W. "Syllabic [n,l]," *QJS* 48.151-6 (1962).

20 AIKEN, Janet Rankin. *Why English Sounds Change.* New York: Ronald Press, 1929.

21 ALGEO, John. "Unrounded back vowels in American English," *MPhon* 116.29-31 (1961).

22 ARMSTRONG, L. E., and I. C. WARD. *Handbook of English Intonation,* 2d edition. London: Heffer, 1939.

23 ARNOLD, G. F. "Stress in English words," *Lingua* 6.221-67, 397-441 (1957).

24 BERGER, Marshall D. "Neutralization in American English vowels," *Word* 5.255-7 (1949).

1 BERGER, Marshall D. "Vowel distribution and accentual prominence in Modern English," *Word* 11.361-76 (1955).

2 BOWEN, J. Donald. "A pedagogical transcription of English," *LL* 10.103-14 (1960).

3 BRONSTEIN, Arthur J. *The Pronunciation of American English.* New York: Appleton-Century-Crofts, 1960.

4 BRONSTEIN, Arthur J. "Some unresolved phonetic-phonemic symbolization problems," *QJS* 47.54-9 (1961).

5 BUCHANAN, Cynthia D. *A Programed Introduction to Linguistics: Phonetics and Phonemics.* Boston: D. C. Heath, 1963. [Reviewed by William E. Castle, *Linguistics* 12.60-6 (1965).]

6 EISENSON, Jon, S. SOUCHER, and J. FISHER. "The affective value of English speech sounds," *QJS* 26.589-94 (1940) .

7 ELIASON, Norman E. "The short vowels in French loan words like *city,*" *Anglia* 63.73-87 (1939).

8 FLETCHER, Harvey. *Speech and Hearing in Communication,* revised edition. New York: Van Nostrand, 1953.

9 FRENCH, N. R., C. W. CARTER, Jr., and Walter KOENIG, Jr. *The Words and Sounds of Telephone Conversations.* (Bell Telephone System Technical Publications, Monograph B-491). New York: Bell Telephone System, 1930.

10 GIMSON, A. C. *An Introduction to the Pronunciation of English.* London: Arnold, 1962. [Reviewed by Arthur Fowler, *Linguistics* 12.72-9 (1965).]

11 GIMSON, A. C. "The linguistic relevance of stress in English," *ZPSK* 9.143-9 (1956).

12 GIMSON, A. C. "Phonetic change and the RP vowel system," *In Honour of Daniel Jones* [5.11], 131-36.

13 HIRSH, I. J. "A brief history of the systems used to represent English sounds," *QJS* 29.334-42 (1943).

14 HOUSEHOLDER, Fred W., Jr. "Unreleased ptk in American English," *For Roman Jakobson* [5.16], 235-44.

15 HULTZÉN, Lee S. "Symbol for the nonsyllabic postvocalic *r* in General American: an essay in phonetic methodology," *QJS* 36.189-201 (1950).

16 JONES, Daniel. *An Outline of English Phonetics,* 9th edition. Cambridge, Eng.: Heffer, 1960.*

17 JONES, Daniel. *The Pronunciation of English,* 4th ed. Cambridge: Cambridge Univ. Press, 1956.

18 JONES, Daniel. "The use of syllabic and nonsyllabic *l* and *n* in derivatives of English words ending in syllabic *l* and *n,*" *Zeitschrift für Phonetik* 12.136-44 (1959).

19 KENYON, John S. *American Pronunciation,* 10th edition. Ann Arbor: Wahr, 1950.*

20 KINGDON, Roger. *The Groundwork of English Intonation.* London: Longmans, Green, 1958.

21 KINGDON, Roger. *The Groundwork of English Stress.* London: Longmans, Green, 1958.

22 KRAPP, George Philip. *The Pronunciation of Standard English in America.* New York: Oxford Univ. Press, 1919.

23 KRUISINGA, Etsko. *An Introduction to the Study of English Sounds,* 11th edition. Rev. by C. Hedeman and J. J. Westerbeek. Groningen: P. Noordhoff, 1957.*

1   KRUISINGA, Etsko. *The Phonetic Structure of English Words*. Bern: Franke, 1943.

2   KURATH, Hans. *A Phonology and Prosody of Modern English*. Ann Arbor: Univ. of Michigan Press, 1964.*

3   LEHMANN, Winfred P. "A note on the change of American English /t/," *AS* 28:4.271-5 (1953).

4   MACLAY, Howard, and Charles E. OSGOOD. "Hesitation phenomena in spontaneous English speech," *Word* 15.19-44 (1959).

5   MALÉCOT, André. "Nasal syllabics in American English," *SL* 14.47-56 (1960). [Reply by Bertil Malmberg, *SL* 15.1-9 (1961).]

6   MALÉCOT, André. "Vowel nasality as a distinctive feature in American English," *Lang* 36.222-9 (1960).

7   MARCHAND, Hans. "Motivation by linguistic form; English ablaut and rime combinations and their relevancy to word-formation," *SN* 29.54-66 (1957).

8   PIKE, Kenneth. *The Intonation of American English*. Ann Arbor: Univ. of Michigan Press, 1944.*

9   PILCH, Herbert. "The rise of the American English vowel pattern," *Word* 11.57-93 (1955).

10   QUIRK, Randolph, *et al.* "Studies in the correspondence of prosodic to grammatical features in English," *P9ICL* [6.15], 679-91.

11   ROBSON, Ernest M. *The Orchestra of the Language*. New York: Thos. Yoseloff, 1959.

12   SCHUBIGER, Maria. *English Intonation, Its Form and Function* (with two phonograph records). Tübingen: Biemeyer, 1958.

13   SHEN, Yao, and Giles G. PETERSON. *Isochronism in English. SILOP* No. 9, 1962.

14   SIGURD, Bengt. "Rank order of consonants established by distributional criteria," *SL* 9.8-20 (1955).

15   STIRLING, W. F. "The transcription of English," *Maître Phonétique* 102.26-28 (1954).

16   THOMAS, Charles Kenneth. *An Introduction to the Phonetics of American English*, 2nd edition. New York: Ronald Press, 1958.

17   WARD, Ida Caroline. *The Phonetics of English*, 4th edition. Cambridge, England: W. Heffer & Sons, 1945.

SYNTAX

See also **2.7, 5.3-4, 74.15, 74.17, 75.3-4, 86.**18, **87.**11, *Syntax*, p. **36** and *Compounds*, p. **75.**

18   ANTHONY, Edward M., Jr. "An exploratory inquiry into lexical clusters," *AS* 29.175-80 (1954).

19   BARBER, C. L. "Some measurable characteristics of modern scientific prose," *Contributions to English Syntax and Philology* [5.3], 21-43.

20   BECKER, Selwyn W., Alex BAVELAS, and Marcia BRADEN. "An index to measure contingency of English sentences," *L&S* 4.139-45 (1961).

21   BEHRE, Frank. *Meditative-Polemic "Should" in Modern English "That"-Clauses.* (*GothSE* no. 4). Stockholm: Almqvist & Wiksell, 1955.

22   BEHRE, Frank. "Notes on indicative clauses of condition," *Contributions to English Syntax and Philology* [5.3], 45-86.

23   BODELSEN, Carl Adolf G. "The expanded tenses in Modern English: an attempt at an explanation," *Englische Studien* 71.220-38 (1936).

1 BODELSEN, Carl Adolf G. "The system governing the use of futuric *shall* and *will*," *SN* 14.393-411 (1941–42).

2 BOLINGER, Dwight L. *Interrogative Structures of American English: The Direct Question. (PADS* no. 28) University: Univ. of Alabama Press, 1957.*

3 BOLINGER, Dwight L. "Syntactic blends and other matters," *Lang* 37.366-81 (1961).

4 BOWMAN, Elizabeth. "The clasification of imperative sentences in English," *SIL* 17.23-8 (1963).

5 BRORSTRÖM, Sverker. *The Increasing Frequency of the Preposition "about" during the Modern English Period.* (Stockholm Studies in English, Vol. 9). Stockholm: Almqvist & Wiksell, 1963.

6 CHARLESTON, Britta M. *Studies on the Syntax of the English Verb.* (Swiss Studies in English). Bern: Verlag A. Franke Ag., 1941.

7 CHARNLEY. M. Bertens. "The syntax of deferred prepositions," *AS* 24.268-77 (1949).

8 CHATMAN, Seymour. "English sentence connectors," *Fries Studies* [**6.11**], 315-34.

9 CHATMAN, Seymour. "Pre-adjectivals in the English nominal phrase," *AS* 35.83-100 (1960).

10 CHRISTOPHERSEN, Paul. *The Articles: A Study of their Theory and Use in English.* Copenhagen: Einar Munksgaard; London: Oxford Univ. Press, 1939.

11 CURME, George O. *Syntax.* Boston: D. C. Heath, 1931.*

12 DENNIS, Leah. "The progressive tense: frequency of its use in English," *PMLA* 55.855-65 (1940).

13 DIVER, William. "The chronological system of the English verb," *Word* 19.141-81 (1963).

14 DIVER, William. "The modal system of the English verb," *Word* 20.322-52 (1964).

15 FRIES, Charles C. "The periphrastic future with 'shall' and 'will' in Modern English," *PMLA* 40.963-1024 (1925).*

16 FRIES, Charles C. *The Structure of English.* New York: Harcourt, Brace and World, 1952.*

17 GAMMON, Edward R. "A statistical study of English syntax," *P9ICL* [**6.15**], 37-43.

18 GOEDSCHE, C. Rudolph. "The terminate aspect of the expanded form: its development and its relation to the gerund," *JEGP* 31.469-77 (1932).

19 GUNTER, Richard. "Elliptical sentences in American English," *Lingua* 12.137-50 (1963).

20 HATCHER, Anna G. "The English construction *A friend of mine*," *Word* 6.1-25 (1950).

21 HATCHER, Anna G. "To get/be invited," *MLN* 64.433-6 (1949).

22 HATCHER, Anna Granville. "The use of the progressive form in English," *Lang* 29.254-80 (1951).

23 HAUGEN, Einar. "On resolving the close apposition," *AS* 28.165-70 (1953).

24 IVES, Sumner. "Hierarchies of determinism in English structure," *GL* 1.14-21 (1955).

25 JACOBSON, Sven. *Adverbial Positions in English.* Stockholm: A. B. Studentbok, 1964.

1   JESPERSEN, Otto. *Analytic Syntax*. London: Allen and Unwin, 1937.

2   KALOGJERA, Damir. "On the relative frequency of *will* and *shall* in questions in the first person," *MSpr* 61.394-7 (1962).

3   KARLSEN, Rolf. *Studies in the Connection of Clauses in Current English: Zero Ellipsis, and Explicit Form*. Bergen: J. W. Eides Bocktryckerei, 1959.

4   KIRCH, Max S. "Scandinavian influence on English syntax," *PMLA* 74.503-10 (1959).

5   KIRCHNER, Gustav. "Recent American influence on standard English: the syntactical sphere," *ZAA* 5.29-42 (1957).

6   KIRCHNER, Gustav. "Verbal 'ing' resumed by an auxiliary," *ES* 43.20-28 (1962).

7   LONG, Ralph B. "The clause patterns of contemporary English," *AS* 32.12-30 (1957).

8   LONG, Ralph B. "The function of complement in the English sentence," *University of Texas Studies in English* 37.127-40 (1958).

9   LONG, Ralph B. *The Sentence and Its Parts: A Grammar of Contemporary English*. Chicago: Univ. of Chicago Press, 1961.

10   MARCHAND, Hans. "Compound and pseudo-compound verbs in present-day English," *AS* 32.83-94 (1957).

11   MARCKWARDT, Albert H. "*Have got* in expressions of possession and obligation," *CE* 16.309-10 (1955).

12   McDAVID, Virginia. "The alternation of 'that' and zero in noun clauses," *AS* 39.102-13 (1964).

13   MÜLLER, Daniel. *Studies in Modern English Syntax: Two Aspects of Synthesis. Part I: Anticipatory Word-Order; Part 2: Deferment of the Preposition, a Phenomenon of Condensation*. Winterthur: P. G. Keller, 1957.

14   MULDEN, G. "The infinitive after *to dare*," *Neophil* 22.25-48 (1936).

15   MUTT, O. "The adjectivization of nouns in English," *ZAA* 12.341-9 (1964).

16   NIDA, Eugene A. *A Synopsis of English Syntax*. Norman, Okla.: Summer Institute of Linguistics, 1960.*

17   OLSSON, Yngve. *On the Syntax of the English Verb, with Special Reference to "Have a Look" and Similar Complex Structures*. (GothSE, 12) Göteborg: Almqvist & Wiksell, 1961.

18   ONIONS, C. T. *An Advanced English Syntax,* 3d edition. London: Kegan Paul, Trench, & Trubner, 1911.

19   OSSELTON, N. E., and C. J. OSSELTON-BLEEKER. "The plural attributive in contemporary English," *ES* 43.476-84 (1962).

20   OWEN, Edward T. "Syntax of the adverb, preposition and conjunction," *TWA* 26.167-221 (1931).

21   PITTMAN, Richard S. "A formula for the English verb auxiliaries," *LL* 12.79-80 (1962).

22   QUIRK, Randolph. "Relative clauses in educated spoken English," *ES* 38.97-109 (1957).

23   ROBERTS, Paul. *English Sentences*. New York: Harcourt, Brace & World, 1962.

24   ROBERTS, Paul. *Patterns of English*. New York: Harcourt, Brace & World, 1956.

25   SALMON, Vivian. "Sentence-types in modern English," *Anglia* 81:23-55 (1963).

1 SCHEURWEGHS, Gustave. *Present-day English Syntax: A Survey of Sentence Patterns.* London: Longmans, Green, 1959.

2 SCHUBIGER, Maria. "The expanded forms of the verb and intonation," *ES* 40.308-13 (1959).

3 SÖDERLIND, Johannes. "Zero-form v. the-form: a study of modern brevity," *Contributions to English Syntax and Philology* [**5**.3], 99-117.

4 SØRENSEN, Holger Steen. "The function of the definite article in modern English," *ES* 40.401-20 (1959).

5 TWADDELL, W. Freeman. *The English Verb Auxiliaries.* Providence, R.I.: Brown Univ. Press, 1960.*

6 VAN ROEY, J. "A note on noun + noun combinations in modern English," *ES* 45.48-52 (1964).

7 VISSER, F. T. "Two or more auxiliaries with a common verbal complement," *ES* 31.11-27 (1950).

American English

GENERAL

See also **2**.18, **3**.2, **3**.13, **3**.16, **3**.20, **4**.15, **27**.1, **72**.15, **80**.9, **85**.15, and **86**.4.

8 BABCOCK, C. Merton. "The social significance of the language of the American frontier," *AS* 24.256-63 (1949).

9 ELIASON, Norman E. "The study of American English," *ES* 39.154-62 (1958).

10 HOLLIS, C. Carroll. "Whitman and the American idiom," *QJS* 43.408-20 (1957).

11 KRAPP, George Philip. *The English Language in America,* 2 vols. New York: Appleton-Century-Crofts, 1925. 2nd edition, New York: Ungar, 1960.*

12 LLOYD, Donald A., and Harry R. WARFEL. *American English in Its Cultural Setting.* New York: Knopf, 1956.

13 MARCKWARDT, Albert H. *American English.* New York: Oxford Univ. Press, 1958. [Ox]

14 MATHEWS, Mitford M., ed. *The Beginnings of American English: Essays and Comments.* Chicago: Univ. of Chicago Press, 1931 [Phoen P123]

15 McDAVID, Raven I., Jr. "American English," *CE* 25.331-7 (1964).

16 MENCKEN, Henry L. *The American Language: The Fourth Edition and the Two Supplements.* Abridged and ed. by Raven I. McDavid, Jr. New York: Knopf, 1963.*

17 NEUMANN, Joshua H. "The Dutch element in the vocabulary of American English," *JEGP* 44.274-80 (1945).

18 POUND, Louise. *Selected writings of Louise Pound.* Lincoln: Univ. of Nebraska Press, 1949.

19 PYLES, Thomas. *Words and Ways of American English.* New York: Random House, 1952. [RH x450] *

20 READ, Allen Walker. "Amphi-Atlantic English," *ES* 17.161-78 (1935).

21 READ, Allen Walker. "The assimilation of the speech of British immigrants in Colonial America," *JEGP* 27.70-9 (1928).

22 READ, Allen Walker. "British recognition of American speech in the eighteenth century," *Dialect Notes* 6:6.313-34 (1933).

1 ROBERTSON, Stuart. "British-American differentiation in syntax and idiom," *AS* 14.243-54 (1939).

2 SHOEMAKER, Robert W. "The nineteenth century: watershed of American religious appellatives," *AS* 34.5-10 (1959).

3 THORNTON, Richard H. *An American Glossary: Being an Attempt to Illustrate Certain Americanisms upon Historical Principles,* with introd. by Margaret M. Bryant. 3 vols. (Reissue of the 1912 two-volume glossary with a volume of additional material first published in Dialect Notes, Vol. 6 (1928–39).) New York: Frederick Ungar, 1962.

DIALECTS

See also 2.12, 4.16, 25.2, 33.17, 33.23-24, 34.1, 34.6, 34.9, 76.8, 80.13, 84.13, 84.24, 85.1, WORD STUDIES ..., p. 66, *Cant,* ... p. 73, and *Linguistic Geography,* p. 81.

4 ALLEN, Harold B. "Aspects of the linguistic geography of the Upper Midwest," Fries *Studies* [6.11], 303-14; also in *RAEL* [5.1], 231-41, as "The primary dialect areas of the Upper Midwest."

5 ALLEN, Harold B. "Minor dialect areas of the Upper Midwest," *PADS* 30.3-16 (1958).

6 ATWOOD, E. Bagby. *"Grease* and *greasy:* a study of geographical variation," *Studies in English,* Univ. of Texas (1950), 249-60. Also in *RAEL* [5.1], 242-51.

7 ATWOOD, E. Bagby. "The pronunciation of 'Mrs.'," *AS* 25.10-18 (1950).

8 ATWOOD, E. Bagby. *The Regional Vocabulary of Texas.* Austin: Univ. of Texas Press, 1962.

9 ATWOOD, E. Bagby. *A Survey of Verb Forms in the Eastern United States.* Studies in American English, No. 2. Ann Arbor: Univ. of Michigan Press, 1953.*

10 AVIS, Walter S. *"Crocus Bag:* A problem in areal linguistics," *AS* 30.5-16 (1955).

11 BLOK, H. P. "Annotations to Mr. Turner's 'Africanisms in the Gullah dialect'," *Lingua* 8:306-21 (1959). See **60**.11.

12 CARRANCO, Lynwood, and Wilma Rawles SIMMONS. "The Boonville Language of Northern California," *As* 39.278-86 (1964).

13 CASSIDY, Frederic G. *A Method for Collecting Dialect. PADS* No. 20 (1953).

14 CASSIDY, Frederic G. "Report on a recent project of collecting: the vocabulary of marble playing," *PADS* 29.28-41 (1958). See also **73**.11.

15 CLARK, Joseph D. "Folk speech from North Carolina," *North Carolina Folklore* 10:6-21 (1962).

16 DAVIS, Alva L., and Raven I. McDAVID, Jr. "Northwestern Ohio: a transition area," *Lang* 26.264-73 (1950).

17 DECAMP, David. "The pronunciation of English in San Francisco," *Orbis* 7.372-91 (1958); 8.54-77 (1959).

18 ELIASON, Norman E. *Tarheel Talk: An Historical Study of the English Language in North Carolina to 1860.* Chapel Hill: Univ. of North Carolina Press, 1956.

19 GREET, W. Cabell. "Southern speech," *Culture in the South,* W. T. Couch, ed. Chapel Hill: Univ. of North Carolina Press, 1934, 594-615.

20 HALE, Edward Everett. "The speech of the frontier," *QJS* 27.353-63 (1941).

21 HALL, Joseph S. *The Phonetics of Great Smoky Mountain Speech. (AS,* Reprints and Monographs No. 4). New York, 1942.

1   HANKEY, Clyde T. *A Colorado Word Geography. PADS* 34 (1960).

2   HANKEY, Clyde T. "Semantic features and eastern relices in Colorado dialect," *AS* 36.266-70 (1961).

3   HANLEY, Miles L. "Observations on the broad A," *Dialect Notes* 5.347-50 (1925).

4   HUBBELL, Allan F. " 'Curl' and 'coil' in New York City," *AS* 15.372-6 (1940.)

5   HUBBELL, Allan F. *The Pronunciation of English in New York City: Consonants and Vowels.* New York: King's Crown Press, 1950.

6   IVES, Sumner. "Pronunciation of *can't* in the Eastern states," *AS* 28.149-57 (1953).

7   KIMBALL, Arthur G. "Sears-Roebuck and regional terms," *AS* 38.209-13 (1963).

8   KIMMERLE, Marjorie. "The influence of locale and human activity on some words in Colorado," *AS* 25.161-7 (1950).

9   KURATH, Hans. "Linguistic regionalism," 297-310 in Merril Jensen, ed., *Regionalism in America,* Madison, Wis.: Univ. of Wisconsin Press (1951).

10 KURATH, Hans. *Word Geography of the Eastern United States.* Ann Arbor: Univ. of Michigan Press, 1949.*

11 KURATH, Hans, and Raven I. McDAVID, Jr. *The Pronunciation of English in the Atlantic States.* Ann Arbor: Univ. of Michigan Press, 1961.*

12 KURATH, Hans (director and editor), *et al. Linguistic Atlas of New England,* 3 vols. in 6 (sponsored by the American Council of Learned Societies and assisted by Universities and Colleges in New England). Providence, R.I.: Brown Univ. 1939-43.* See also **82**.6.

13 LINDBLAD, Karl-Erik. *Noah Webster's Pronunciation and Modern New England Speech.* Cambridge: Harvard Univ. Press, 1955.

14 MARCKWARDT, Albert H. "Principal and subsidiary dialect areas in the North Central States," *PADS* No. 27.3-15 (1957). Also in *RAEL* [**5**.1], 220-30.

15 McDAVID, Raven I., Jr. "American English Dialects," *The Structure of American English* [**49**.3], 480-543.

16 McDAVID, Raven I., Jr. "Postvocalic /-r/ in South Carolina: a social analysis," *AS* 23.194-203 (1948).

17 McDAVID, Raven I., Jr. "The second round in dialectology of North American English," *JCLA* 6.108-15 (1960).

18 McDAVID, Raven I., Jr., and Virginia McDAVID. "Grammatical differences in the North Central States," *AS* 35.5-19 (1960).

19 McDAVID, Raven I., Jr., and Virginia McDAVID. "Regional linguistic atlases in the United States," *Orbis* 5.349-86 (1956).

20 McDAVID, Raven I., Jr., and Virginia McDAVID. "The relation of the speech of American Negroes to the speech of the whites," *AS* 26.3-17 (1951).

21 MILLER, Virginia R. "Present-day use of the broad A in Eastern Massachusetts," *SM* 20.235-46 (1953).

22 NORMAN, Arthur M. Z. "A Southeast Texas dialect study," *Orbis* 5.61-79 (1956).

23 PEARCE, T. M. "Three Rocky Mountain terms: *park, sugan,* and *plaza,*" *AS* 33.99-107 (1958).

24 PENZL, Herbert. "The vowel-phonemes in *father, man, dance* in dictionaries and New England speech," *JEGP* 39.13-32 (1940).

1 RANDOLPH, Vance, and George P. WILSON. *Down in the Holler: a Gallery of Ozark Folk Speech*. Norman: Univ. of Oklahoma Press, 1953.

2 REED, Carroll E. "The pronunciation of English in the Pacific Northwest," *Lang* 37.559-64 (1961).

3 REED, Carroll E. "Washington Words," *PADS* 25.3-11 (1956).

4 REED, David W. "Eastern dialect words in California," *PADS* 21.3-15 (1954).

5 ROWE, H. D. "New England terms for *bull*," *AS* 32.110-16 (1957).

6 SHUY, Roger W. *The Northern-Midland Dialect Boundary in Illinois*. *PADS* 38, 1962.

7 STANLEY, Oma. *The Speech of East Texas*. *AS*, Monograph No. 2. New York: Columbia Univ. Press, 1937.

8 THOMAS, Charles K. "The linguistic Mason and Dixon line," 251-55 in Donald C. Bryant, ed., *The Rhetorical Idiom*. Ithaca, N.Y.: Cornell Univ. Press, 1958.

9 THOMAS, Charles K. "The phonology of New England English," *SM* 28.223-32 (1961).

10 THOMAS, Charles K. "The place of New York City in American linguistic geography," *QJS* 33.314-20 (1947).

11 TURNER, Lorenzo D. *Africanisms in the Gullah Dialect*. Chicago: Univ. of Chicago Press, 1949.

12 WALSER, Richard. "Negro dialect in eighteenth-century American drama," *AS* 30.269-76 (1955).

13 WETMORE, Thomas H. *The Low-central and Low-back Vowels in the English of the Eastern United States*. *PADS* 32, 1959.

14 WHEATLEY, Katherine E., and Oma STANLEY. "Three generations of East Texas speech," *AS* 34.83-94 (1959).

15 WHITEHALL, Harold. "The orthography of John Bate of Sharon, Connecticut (1700–1784)," *AS* 22:1, Pt. 2, 3-56 (1947).

16 WOOD, Gordon R. "Dialect contours in the southern states," *AS* 38.243-56 (1963).

British English and American English

See also **4**.9 and **85**.15.

17 CAREY, G. V. *American into English: a Handbook for Translators*. London: Heinemann, 1953.

18 EKWALL, Eilert. "American and British pronunciation," *SN* 18.161-90 (1945–46).

19 FLASDIECK, Hermann M. "British pyjamas—American pajama(s)," *Anglia* 69.239-63 (1950).

20 FOSTER, Brian. "Recent American influence on standard English," *Anglia* 73.328-60 (1956).

21 KILBY, Clyde. "Signs in Great Britain," *WSt* 31.7 (1955).

22 LEE, W. R. "Some features of the intonation of questions," *Eng. Lang. Teaching* 10:66-70 (1956).

23 LOHRLI, Anne. "*Knocked up* in England and the United States," *AS* 35.24-28 (1960).

24 NOVAK, Benjamin J. "The queen's English," *EJ* 53.360-1 (1964).

1 SÖDERLIND, Johannes. "Notes on received English pronunciation," *SN* 31.191-94 (1959).

British English Dialects

See also **3**.8, **4**.19, **34**.11, **83**.16, **83**.20, and *Linguistic Geography*, p. **81**.

2 ARNOLD, G. F. "Strong and weak forms in Southern British English," *MPhon* 113.5-7 (1960).

3 BROOK, G. L. *English Dialects*. London: André Deutsch, 1963.

4 DIETH, Eugene. "A survey of English dialects," *E&S* 32.74-104 (1947).

5 FRANCIS, W. Nelson. "Some dialect glosses in England," *AS* 34.243-50 (1959).

6 FRANCIS, W. Nelson. "Some dialectal verb forms in England," *Orbis* 10.1-14 (1961).

7 FRANKLYN, Julian. *The Cockney: a Survey of London Life and Language*. London: André Deutsch, 1953.

8 JACOBSSON, Ulf. *Phonological Dialect Constituents in the Vocabulary of Standard English*. LSE 31. Lund: Gleerup, 1962.

9 KÖKERITZ, Helge. *The Phonology of the Suffolk Dialect: Descriptive and Historical*. Uppsala: Lundequistska Bokhandeln, 1932.

10 KOLB, Edward. "The icicle in English dialects," *ES* 40.238-88 (1959).

11 MATTHEWS, William. *Cockney Past and Present: A Short History of the Dialect of London*. New York: E. P. Dutton, 1938.

12 MOORE, Samuel, Sanford B. MEECH, and Harold WHITEHALL. "Middle English Dialect Characteristics and Dialect Boundaries," *Essays and Studies in English and Comparative Literature*, UMPLL 13.1-60 (1935).

13 SIVERTSEN, Eva. *Cockney Phonology*. OSE no. 8. Oslo: Univ. Press, 1960.

14 SKEAT, Walter W. *English Dialects from the Eighth Century to the Present Day*. England: Cambridge Univ. Press, 1912.*

Commonwealth English: Australia, Canada, Jamaica, South Africa

See also **1**.20, **2**.14, **73**.21, and **78**.22.

15 ALLEN, Harold B. "Canadian-American speech differences along the middle border," *JCLA* 5.17-24 (1959).

16 AVIS, Walter S. "A bibliography of writings on Canadian English," *JCLA* 1.19-20 (1955).

17 AVIS, Walter S. "Canadian English merits a dictionary," *Culture* 18.245-56 (1957).

18 AVIS, Walter S. "Linguistica Canadiana: Canadian English," *JCLA* 2.82 (1956).

19 AVIS, Walter S. "Speech differences along the Ontario-United States border," *JCLA* 1.13-19 (1954); "Grammar and syntax," 1.14-19 reg. series (1955); "Pronunciation," 2.41-59 (1956).

20 BAKER, Sidney John. "Australian English," *The Australian Encyclopedia*, ed. A. H. Chisholm, vol. 1. East Lansing, Mich.: Michigan State Univ. Press, 1958.

21 BLOOMFIELD, Morton W. "Canadian English and its relation to eighteenth century American speech," *JEGP* 47.59-67 (1948).

62 ENGLISH LANGUAGE & LINGUISTICS

1 BRECKWOLDT, G. H. "Some aspects of the phonetics of vowels in South African English," *MPhon* 115.5-12 (1961).

2 CASSIDY, Frederic G. *Jamaica Talk: Three Hundred Years of the English Language in Jamaica.* New York: St. Martin's Press, 1961.*

3 DEAN, Christopher. "Is there a distinctive literary Canadian English?" *AS* 38.278-82 (1963).

4 GREGG, R. J. "Neutralization and fusion of vocalic phonemes in Canadian English as spoken in the Vancouver area," *JCLA* 3.78-83 (1957).

5 HAMILTON, Donald E. "Notes on Montreal English," *JCLA* 4.70-79 (1958).

6 HAMILTON, Donald E. "Standard Canadian English: Pronunciation," *P9ICL* [6.15], 456-59.

7 JOOS, Martin. "A phonological dilemma in Canadian English," *Lang* 18.141-4 (1942).

8 KNOWLES-WILLIAMS, G., *et al.* "English in South Africa, 1960," *ESA* 4.63-98 (1961).

9 LEHN, Walter. "Vowel contrasts in a Saskatchewan English dialect," *JCLA* 5.90-98 (1959).

10 PORTER, Bernard H. "A Newfoundland vocabulary," *AS* 38.297-301 (1963).

11 SCARGILL, M. H. "Canadian English and Canadian culture in Alberta," *JCLA* 1.26-30 (1955).

12 SCARGILL, M. H. "Sources of Canadian English," *JEGP* 56.610-14 (1957).

13 STORY, G. M. "Research in the language and place-names of Newfoundland," *JCLA* 3.47-55 (1957).

14 WIDDOWSON, J. D. A. "Some items of a central Newfoundland dialect," *CJL* 10:1.37-46 (1964).

Usage

GENERAL

See also 3.2, 3.4, 34.12, 79.17, 79.19, 80.7-8, and 80.20.

15 BAKER, R. J. "The 'linguistic' theory of usage," *JCLA* 6.209-12 (1961). Also in *RAEL* [5.1], 303-6.

16 BEAUCHAMP, Emerson, Jr. "A study of 'it': handbook treatment and magazine use," *AS* 26.173-80 (1951).

17 BERRY, Edmund G. "Clichés and their sources," *MLN* 59.50-2 (1944).

18 BLOOMFIELD, Leonard. "Secondary and tertiary responses to language," *Lang* 20.45-55 (1944).*

19 BRYANT, Margaret M., ed. *Current American Usage.* New York: Funk & Wagnalls, 1962.

20 CANNON, Charles D. "A survey of the subjunctive mood in English," *AS* 34.11-19 (1959).

21 CHRISTENSEN, Francis. "Number concord with 'what'-clauses again," *AS* 33.226-9 (1958).

22 ERICSON, E. E. "Noun clauses in 'because'," *Anglia* 61.112-3 (1937).

23 FRANCIS, W. Nelson. "A standard corpus of edited present-day American English," *CE* 26.267-73 (1965).

24 FRIES, Charles C. "The rules of common school grammars," *PMLA* 42.221-37 (1927).*

1 GUERARD, Albert. "Ten levels of language," *ASch* 16.148-58 (1947).

2 HARTUNG, Charles V. "Doctrines of English usage," *EJ* 45.517-25 (1956).

3 HILL, Archibald A. "Correctness and style in English composition," *CE* 12.280-85 (1951).

4 HILL, Archibald A. "Prescriptivism and linguistics in English teaching," *CE* 15.395-9 (1954).

5 HORNBY, A. S. *A Guide to Patterns and Usage in English*. London: Oxford Univ. Press, 1954.

6 JOOS, Martin. *The Five Clocks. IJAL* 28, No. 2 (1962).*

7 KENNEDY, Arthur G. *English Usage*. Monograph No. 15, NCTE. New York: Appleton-Century-Crofts, 1942.

8 KENYON, John S. "Cultural levels and functional varieties of English," *CE* 10.31-36 (1948). Also in *RAEL* [5.1], 294-301.

9 KNOTT, Thomas A. "Standard English and incorrect English," *AS* 9.83-9 (1934).

10 KÖKERITZ, Helge. "Spelling-pronunciation in American English," *In Honour of Daniel Jones* [5.11], 137-45.

11 LAMBERTS, J. J. "Another look at Kenyon's levels," *CE* 24.141-3 (1962).

12 LEONARD, Sterling A. *Current English Usage*. (Monograph No. 1.) Chicago: National Council of Teachers of English, 1932.*

13 MALMSTROM, Jean. "Linguistic Atlas findings *versus* textbook pronouncements on current American usage," *EJ* 48.191-98 (1959). Also in *RAEL* [5.1], 316-24.

14 MARCKWARDT, Albert H., and Fred WALCOTT. *Facts about Current English Usage*. Monograph No. 7, NCTE. New York: Appleton-Century-Crofts, 1938.*

15 RYAN, William M. "Pseudo-subjunctive 'were'," *AS* 36.48-53 (1961); "More on pseudo-subjunctive 'were'," 37.114-22 (1962).

16 SCOTT, Fred Newton. *The Standard of American Speech and Other Papers*. Boston, New York, etc.: Allyn & Bacon, 1926. [Review: A. G. Kennedy in *AS* 1.618 (1926).]

17 STREVENS, P. D. "Varieties of English," *ES* 45.20-30 (1964).

18 THOMAS, Russell. "Notes on the inflected genitive in modern American prose," *CE* 14.236-39 (1953).

19 ULVESTAD, Bjarne. "An approach to describing usage of language variants," *Memoir 12, IJAL* (Suppl. to 22:1) 37-59 (IUPAL.) Baltimore, 1956.

20 WINTER, Werner. "Styles as dialects," *P9ICL* [6.15], 324-30.

HISTORY OF ATTITUDES TOWARD USAGE

See also **34**.15 and **80**.12.

21 BERGENHAN, Mildred E. "The doctrine of correctness in English usage in the nineteenth century," *Summaries of Doctoral Dissertations,* Univ. of Wisconsin (n.d.) 4.230-32 (1940).

22 BREDE, Alexander. "The idea of an English language academy," *EJ* (Coll. Ed.) 26.560-8 (1937).

23 BRONSTEIN, Arthur J. "Nineteenth-century attitudes towards pronunciation," *QJS* 40.417-21 (1954).

24 CONGELTON, J. E. "Historical development of the concept of rhetorical proprieties," *CCC* (NCTE) 5.14-45 (1954).

1 EMSLEY, Bert. "James Buchanan and the eighteenth century regulation of English usage," *PMLA* 48.1154-66 (1933).

2 LEONARD, Sterling A. *The Doctrine of Correctness in English Usage 1700–1800.* Madison: Univ. of Wisconsin Studies in Language and Literature, No. 25, 1929.*

3 READ, Allen Walker. "American projects for an academy to regulate speech," *PMLA* 51.1141-79 (1936).

4 READ, Allen Walker. "Suggestions for an academy in England in the latter half of the eighteenth century," *MP* 36.145-56 (1938).

5 SHELDON, Esther K. "Standards of English pronunciation according to the grammarians and orthoepists of the 16th, 17th, and 18th centuries," *Summaries of Doctoral Dissertations,* Univ. of Wisconsin, 3.304-5 (1938).

Vocabulary

GROWTH AND MEASUREMENT

See also **75.9.**

6 DIKE, Edwin B. "Our obsolete vocabulary: some historical views," *PQ* 13.48-55 (1934).

7 ELLEGÅRD, Alvar. "Estimating vocabulary size," *Word* 16.219-44 (1960).

8 FRIES, Charles C., and A. Aileen TRAVER. *English Word Lists.* Washington, D.C.: American Council on Education, 1940.*

9 HERDAN, Gustav. "Relativity of vocabulary ratios," *P8ICL* [6.15], 813-15.

10 HERDAN, Gustav. "Vocabulary statistics and phonology: a parallel," *Lang* 37.247-55 (1961).

11 LEVIN, Saul. "The fallacy of a universal list of basic vocabulary," *P9ICL* [6.15], 232-36.

12 SALLING, Aage. "An essay in comparative vocabulary study," *MLJ* 42.222-25 (1958).

13 THORNDIKE, E. L., and Irving LORGE. *The Teacher's Word Book of Thirty Thousand Words.* New York: Teachers College, 1944.*

14 VOELKER, C. H. "The one-thousand most frequent spoken-words," *QJS* 28.189-98 (1942).

15 WEST, Michael. *A General Service List of English Words: with Semantic Frequencies and a Supplementary Word-list for the Writing of Popular Science and Technology.* London: Longmans, Green, 1953. [Embodies the findings of the Lorge-Thorndike semantic frequency count.] *

16 YULE, G. U. *The Statistical Study of Literary Vocabulary.* New York: Macmillan, 1944.

ENGLISH LOANWORDS IN OTHER LANGUAGES

17 BENSON, Morton. "English loan words in Russian sport terminology," *AS* 33.252-9 (1958).

18 BON, Primus B. "English words in Swiss German usage," *AS* 24.31-7 (1949).

19 BROSNAHAN, L. F. "English in southern Nigeria," *ES* 39.97-110 (1958).

20 BROSNAHAN, L. F. "Some aspects of the linguistic situation in tropical Africa," *Lingua* 12.54-65 (1963).

21 CHARLESTON, Britta M. "The English linguistic invasion of Switzerland," *ES* 40.271-82 (1959).

ENGLISH LANGUAGE & LINGUISTICS **65**

1 FIZIAK, Jacek. "English sports terms in modern Polish," *ES* 45.230-36 (1964).

2 FOWKES, Robert A. "English idiom in modern Welsh," *Word* 1.239-48 (1945).

3 GANG, P. F. "Some English loanwords in Germany," *MLR* 49.478-83 (1954).

4 HALL, Robert A., Jr., "English loan-words in Micronesian languages," *Lang* 21.214-19 (1945).

5 KIRKCONNELL, Watson. *Common English Loanwords in Eastern European Languages.* Slavistica No. 14. Winnipeg, Can.: The Ukrainian Free Academy of Science, 1952.

6 KRAUSS, Paul G. "The Anglo-American influence on German," *AS* 38.257-69 (1963).

7 LANE, Ralph H. "English into Dutch," *GR* 34.235-41 (1959).

8 LEISI, Ernst. "Recent English influences on German meanings," *ES* 40.314-18 (1959).

9 PALMER, P. M. "The influence of English on the German vocabulary to 1880: a supplement," *UCPL* 7:2.39-72 (1960).

10 SCHORER, C. E. "English loan words in Puerto Rico," *AS* 28.22-5 (1953).

11 STENE, Aasta. *English Loan-words in Modern Norwegian: a Study of Linguistic Borrowing in the Process.* London: Oxford Univ. Press, 1945.

12 SWANSON, Donald C. "English loanwords in Modern Greek," *Word* 14.26-46 (1958).

13 ULLMANN, Stephen. "Anglicisms in French—notes on their chronology, range, and reception," *PMLA* 62.1153-77 (1947).

LOANWORDS IN ENGLISH FROM OTHER LANGUAGES

See also 2.16.

14 ALBRECHT, Emil A. "New German words in popular English dictionaries," *GQ* 22.10-16 (1949).

15 ALEXANDER, Henry. "The French element in the English vocabulary," *Culture* 14.274-80 (1953).

16 BARTLETT, Harley Harris. "Malayan words in English," *Michigan Alumnus Quarterly Review* 40.40-55 (1953).

17 BAUGH, Albert C. "The chronology of French loanwords in English," *MLN* 50.90-93 (1935).

18 BENSON, Morton. "Russianisms in the American press," *AS* 37.41-7 (1962).

19 BENTLEY, Harold W. *A Dictionary of Spanish Terms in English: With Special Reference to the American Southwest.* Columbia Univ. Studies in English and Comparative Literature. New York: Columbia Univ. Press, 1932.

20 CARR, Charles T. *The German Influence on the English Vocabulary.* Society for Pure English, Tract No. 42. Oxford: Clarendon Press, 1934.

21 CLARK, G. N. *The Dutch Influence on the English Vocabulary.* Society for Pure English, Tract No. 42. Oxford: Clarendon Press, 1935.

22 DANIELSSON, Bror. *Studies on the Accentuation of Polysyllabic Latin, Greek, and Romance Loanwords in English. With Special Reference to Those Endings in* -able, -ate, -ator, -ible, -ic, -ical, *and* -ize. Stockholm Studies in English. No. 3, edited by Frank Behre. New York: Stechert-Hafner, 1948.

66 ENGLISH LANGUAGE & LINGUISTICS

1   DARYUSH, A. A. "Persian words in English," *Society for Pure English*
    Tract No. 41, pp. 3-20. Oxford: Clarendon Press, 1934.

2   GALINSKY, Hans. "Stylistic aspects of borrowing: a stylistic and com-
    parative view of American elements in Modern German, and American
    English," *P9ICL* [6.15], 374-81.

3   HAUGEN, Einar. "The analysis of linguistic borrowing," *Lang* 26.210-31
    (1950).

4   HOPE, T. E. "Loan-words as cultural and lexical symbols," *ArL* 14.111-21
    (1962); 15.29-42 (1963).

5   JOHNSON, Edwin L. *Latin Words of Common English*. Boston: D. C.
    Heath, 1931.

6   LOGEMAN, H. "Low-Dutch elements in English," *Neophil* 16.31-46, 103-16
    (1930).

7   RAO, G. *Indian Words in English; A Study in Indo-British Cultural and
    Linguistic Relations*. New York: Oxford Univ. Press, 1954.

8   ROCKWELL, Leo L. "German loan words in American English," *Fries
    Studies* [6.11], 229-40.

9   ROSS, Alan S. C. *Ginger, A Loan-Word Study*. Oxford: Blackwell, 1952.

10 SERJEANTSON, Mary S. *A History of Foreign Words in English*. London:
    Routledge and Kegan Paul, 1961; New York: Barnes and Noble, 1961.*

11 SMOCK, John C. *The Greek Element in English Words*. ed. by Percy W.
    Long. New York: Macmillan, 1931.

12 TAYLOR, Walt. "Arabic words in English," *Society for Pure English*, Tract
    No. 38, 567-99 (1933).

13 THOMPSON, J. Eric S. "Pitfalls and stimuli in the interpretation of history
    through loan words," *Philological and Documentary Studies* (Middle
    American Research Institute, Tulane Univ.) Vol. 1 (1943).

14 THORSON, Per. *Anglo-Norse Studies. An Inquiry into the Scandinavian
    Element in the Modern English Dialects*. Part I. Amsterdam: N. V. Swets
    en Zeitlinger, 1936.

WORD STUDIES, PUNS, ACRONYMS, HOMONYMS, ETC.

See also **2.11**, **2.17**, and **5.4**.

15 ALLEN, Hope Emily. "The influence of superstition on vocabulary," *PMLA*
    51.904-20 (1936).

16 ASIMOV, Isaac. *Words of Science, and the History Behind Them*. Boston:
    Houghton, Mifflin, 1959.

17 BAUM, Paull F. "Chaucer's puns," *PMLA* 71.225-46 (1956); "Chaucer's
    puns: a supplementary list," *PMLA* 73.167-70 (1958).

18 BAUM, S. V. "The acronym, pure and impure," *AS* 37.48-50 (1962).

19 BROWN, James. "Eight types of puns," *PMLA* 71.14-26 (1956).

20 DAVIS, Harold Thayer. *The Fine Art of Punning*. Evanston, Ill.: Principia
    Press, 1954.

21 EVANS, Bergen. *Comfortable Words*. New York: Random House, 1962.

22 FELLOWS, Erwin W. "*Propaganda:* history of a word," *AS* 34.182-89 (1959).

23 FLASDIECK, Hermann M. "Pall Mall," *Anglia* 72.129-38 (1954).

1 GREENOUGH, James Bradstreet, and George Lyman KITTREDGE. *Words and Their Ways in English Speech.* New York: Macmillan, 1902, repr. 1922. [Macm MP 65; Bea BP 136.] *

2 JESPERSEN, Otto. *Monosyllables in English.* (Biennial Lecture on English Philology, British Academy.) London: Oxford Univ. Press, 1928.

3 KÖKERITZ, Helge. "Punning names in Shakespeare," *MLN* 65.240-43 (1950).

4 KORNBLUTH, Alice Fox. "Another Chaucer pun," *N&Q* 6.243 (1959).

5 LEVIN, Samuel R. "Homonyms and English form-class analysis," *AS* 35.243-51 (1960).

6 LEWIS, C. S. *Studies in Words.* Cambridge: Univ. Press, 1960.

7 LIPSKI, Patricia W. "The introduction of *Automobile* into American English," *AS* 39.176-87 (1964).

8 LOOMIS, C. G. "Surnames in American wordplay," *Names* 4.86-95 (1956).

9 McKNIGHT, George H. *English Words and Their Background.* New York: Appleton-Century-Crofts, 1923.

10 MENNER, Robert J. "The conflict of homonyms in English," *Lang* 12.229-44 (1936).

11 NYBAKKEN, Oscar E. *Greek and Latin in Scientific Terminology.* Ames, Ia.: Iowa State College Press, 1959.

12 O'CONNOR, J. D. "Phonetic aspects of the spoken pun," *ES* 33.116-24 (1952).

13 READ, Allen Walker. "The first stage in the history of OK," *AS* 38.5-27; "The second stage in the history of OK," 82-102 (1963); "The folklore of OK," 39.5-25; "Later stages in the history of OK," 83-101; "Successive revisions in the explanation of OK," 243-67 (1964).*

14 SCHREUDER, Hindrik. *Pejorative Sense Development in English.* Groningen: Noordhoff, 1929.

15 SHEARD, John A. *The Words We Use.* New York: Praeger, 1954. [Historical study of the literary vocabulary.]

16 SHELDON, Esther K. "Some pun among the hucksters," *AS* 31.13-20 (1956).

17 VAN DONGEN, G. A. *Amelioratives in English.* Rotterdam: De Vries, 1933.

18 WAIN, Harry. *The Story Behind the Word; Some Interesting Origins of Medical Terms.* Springfield, Ill.: C. C. Thomas, 1958.

19 WEEKLEY, Ernest. *Words Ancient and Modern.* New York: Transatlantic Arts, 1947.

20 WELLS, Rulon S. "Acronymy," *For Roman Jakobson* [5.16], 662-67.

21 WILLIAMS, Edna R. *The Conflict of Homonyms in English.* (*YSE* no. 100). New Haven: Yale Univ. Press, 1944.

Language Instruction

General Studies

See also 1.21, 2.2, 5.13, 14.24, 36.14, 72.1, 72.3, 74.13, and *Bilingualism*, p. 72.

22 BROOKS, Nelson. *Language and Language Learning; Theory and Practice.* New York: Harcourt, Brace and World, 1960.*

23 CARROLL, John B. "Linguistic relativity, contrastive linguistics, and language learning," *IRAL* 1.1-20 (1963).

1 CIOFFARI, Vincenzo. "The importance of the printed word in the learning of a foreign language," *MLJ* 46.312-14 (1962).

2 CORDER, S. Pit. "The language laboratory," *English Lang. Teaching* 16.184-88 (1962).

3 DILLER, Edward. "The linguistic sequence in learning foreign languages," *MLJ* 46.259-60 (1962).

4 FRIES, Charles C. "Preparation of teaching materials, practical grammars, and dictionaries, especially for foreign languages," *P8ICL* [6.15]. Repr. in *LL* 9.43-50 (1959).

5 GESSMAN, Albert M. "Another language—another pattern of thinking," *CLAJ* 3.141-53 (1960).

6 GOUIN, François. *The Art of Teaching and Studying Languages*. Tr. by Howard Swan and Victor Bétis, 5th edition. London: G. Philip & Son, 1896.

7 GREEN, Eugene. "On grading phonic interference," *LL* 13.85-96 (1963).

8 HAAS, Mary R. "The linguist as a teacher of languages," *Lang* 19.203-8 (1943).

9 HALLIDAY, M. A. K., Angus MCINTOSH, and Peter STREVENS. *The Linguistic Sciences and Language Teaching*. London: Longmans, Green, 1964; Bloomington: Indiana Univ. Press, 1965.

10 HUEBNER, Theodore. *Audio-Visual Techniques in Teaching Foreign Languages*. New York: New York Univ. Press, 1960.

11 JESPERSEN, Otto. *How to Teach a Foreign Language*. Tr. by Sophia Yhlen-Olsen Bertelsen. London: Allen & Unwin, 1904, repr. 1961.*

12 LADO, Robert. *Language Teaching: A Scientific Approach*. New York: McGraw-Hill, 1964. [Reviewed by Sol Soporta, *Lang* 41.547-51 (1965).] *

13 LADO, Robert. *Linguistics Across Cultures: Applied Linguistics for Language Teachers*. Ann Arbor: Univ. of Michigan Press, 1957.*

14 LAMBERT, Wallace E. "Developmental aspects of second-language acquisition: II. Associational stereotypy, associational form, vocabulary commonness, and pronunciation," *JSP* 43.91-8; III. "A description of developmental changes." 43.88-104 (1956).

15 LAMBERT, Wallace E. "Psychological approaches to the study of language. Pt. I: On learning, thinking and human abilities. Pt. II: On second-language learning and bilingualism," *MLJ* 47.51-62, 114-121 (1963). Also in *TESL* [71.1].

16 LANE, Harlan. "Programmed learning of a second language," *IRAL* 11.249-301 (1964).

17 LANE, Harlan. "Some differences between first and second language learning," *LL* 12.1-14 (1962).

18 LIBBISH, B. *Advances in the Teaching of Modern Languages*. I. Oxford: Pergamon Press, 1964.

19 "Linguistics and language teaching," *IRAL* 11.37-52 (1964). [Report of a working committee of the 1962 Northeast Conference on the Teaching of Foreign Languages.]

20 LIVINGSTONE, Leon. "'Organic' vs. 'functional' grammar in the audiolingual approach," *MLJ* 46. 304-7 (1962).

21 MOULTON, William G. "Applied linguistics in the classroom," *PMLA* 76:2.1-6 (1961). Also in *TESL* [71.1].

22 MOULTON, William G. *Linguistics and Language Teaching in the United States—1940–1960*. Washington: U. S. Government Printing Office, 1962. Also in *Trends* [18.25], 82-109.

1 MOULTON, William G. "What is structural drill?" *Structural Drill* [5.13], 3-15.

2 NIDA, Eugene A. *Learning a Foreign Language.* Revised edition. New York: Friendship Press, 1957.*

3 NIDA, Eugene A. "Some psychological problems in language learning," *LL* 8.7-15 (1958). Also in *TESL* [71.1].

4 POLITZER, Robert L. "On the relationship of linguistics to language teaching," *MLJ* 42.65-8 (1958).

5 PULGRAM, Ernst, ed. *Applied Linguistics in Language Teaching.* (Monograph Series on Languages and Languages and Linguistics, No. 6) Washington, D. C.: Georgetown Univ. Press, 1954.

6 REED, David W., Robert LADO, and Yao SHEN. "The importance of the native language in foreign language learning," *LL* 1:1.17-23 (1948).

7 RIVERS, Wilga M. *The Psychologist and the Foreign Language Teacher.* Chicago: Univ. of Chicago Press, 1964.

8 ST.-CLAIR-SOBELL, James. "Phonology and language teaching," *JCLA* 1:2.14-18 (1955).

9 SHEN, Yao. "Experience classification and linguistic distribution," *LL* 10.1-13 (1960).

10 SHEN, Yao. "Some allophones can be important," *LL* 9.7-18 (1959).

11 STEVICK, Earl W. "Structural drills in the laboratory," *Structural Drill* [5.13], 37-44.

12 SWEET, Henry. *The Practical Study of Languages.* London: Dent, 1899.*

13 TWADDELL, W. Freeman. "Does the foreign-language teacher have to teach English grammar?" *PMLA* 77:2.18-22 (1962).

14 TWADDELL, W. Freeman. "Linguistic research and language teaching," *FR* 33.577-90 (1960).

15 UPSHUR, J. A. "Language proficiency testing and the contrastive analysis dilemma," *LL* 12.123-7 (1962).

16 WEINSTEIN, Ruth Hirsch. "Phonetics, phonemics, and pronunciation: application," *Applied Linguistics* [69.5], 28-38.

English to English Speakers: Grammar, Composition, Etc.

See also **79**.19.

17 BAUGH, Albert C. "Historical linguistics and the teacher of English," *CE* 24.106-10 (1962).

18 BROOKS, Charlotte K. "Some approaches to teaching standard English as a second language," *Elementary English* 41.728-33 (1964).

19 CURME, George O. "Are our teachers of English adequately prepared for their work?" *PMLA* 46.1415-26 (1932).

20 FRANCIS, W. Nelson. "Revolution in grammar," *QJS* 40.299-312 (1954).

21 FRIES, Charles C. *The Teaching of the English Language.* New York: Thos. Nelson & Sons, 1927. [Review, *AS* 3.243-5 (1928), A. G. Kennedy.]

22 GLEASON, H. A., Jr. "What grammar?" *HER* 34.267-81 (1964).

23 GOLDEN, Ruth I. *Improving Patterns of English Usage.* Detroit: Wayne State Univ. Press, 1960.

1   GORRELL, Robert M. "Grammar in the composition course," *CE* 16.232-8 (1955).

2   GOTT, Evelyn. "Teaching regional dialects in junior high school." *EJ* 53.342-4 (1964).

3   HAYAKAWA, S. I. "Linguistic science and the teaching of composition." *ETC.* 7.97-103 (1950).

4   HILL, Archibald A. "Linguistics and the college teacher of language, literature or composition?" *CLAJ* 2.75-86 (1958).

5   HUNT, Kellogg W. "Improving sentence structure." *EJ* 47.206-11 (1958).

6   HUNT, Kellogg W. "A synopsis of clause-to-sentence length factors." *EJ* 54.300-309 (1965).

7   IVES, Sumner. "Grammar and the academic conscience." *CE* 24.98-101 (1962).

8   KURATH, Hans. "Area linguistics and the teacher of English." *LL,* Spec. Issue No. 2.9-12 (1961). Also in *RAEL* [**5.**1], 203-7.

9   LEES, Robert B. "The promise of transformational grammar." *EJ* 52.327-30 (1963).

10   LEVIN, Samuel R. "Comparing traditional and structural grammar." *CE* 21.260-5 (1960). Also in *RAEL* [**5.**1], 46-53.

11   MacCAMPBELL, James C., ed. *Readings in the Language Arts in the Elementary School.* Boston: D. C. Heath, 1964.

12   PIKE, Kenneth L. "A linguistic contribution to composition." *CCC* (NCTE) 15.82-8 (1964).

13   POOLEY, Robert C. *Teaching English Grammar.* New York: Appleton-Century-Crofts, 1957. [Review, James Sledd, *Lang* 34.139-44 (1958).] [Bib.]

14   POOLEY, Robert C. *Teaching English Usage.* New York: Appleton-Century-Crofts, 1946.

15   POUND, Louise. "The value of English linguistics to the teacher," *AS* 1.101-6 (1925).

16   ROBERTS, Paul. "Linguistics and the teaching of composition." *EJ* 52.331-35 (1963).

17   SMITH, Henry Lee, Jr. *Linguistic Science and the Teaching of English* (The Inglis Lecture). Cambridge: Harvard Univ. Press, 1956.

18   STEWART, William A. "Foreign Language Teaching Methods in Quasi-Foreign Language Situations," in *Non-Standard Speech* [**70.**19], 1-15.

19   STEWART, William A., ed. *Non-Standard Speech and the Teaching of English.* Washington: Center for Applied Linguistics, 1964.

20   THOMAS, Owen. "Generative grammar: toward unification and simplification," *EJ* 51.94-99 (1962). Also in *RAEL* [**5.**1], 405-14.

21   WEIR, Ruth Hirsch. "A suggested new direction in primary school language teaching," *Fries Studies* [**6.**11], 343-52.

English to Speakers of Other Languages: English as a Second Language

See also 1.10, 2.3, 69.8-9, and *Bilingualism,* p. **72.**

22   ABERCROMBIE, David. *Problems and Principles: Studies in the Teaching of English as a Second Language.* London, New York, and Toronto: Longmans, Green, 1956.

1 ALLEN, Harold B., ed. *Teaching English as a Second Language: A Book of Readings*. New York: McGraw-Hill, 1965. [Cited herein as *TESL*.]

2 ALLEN, Virginia French, ed. *On Teaching English to Speakers of Other Languages*, Series 1. Papers read at the TESOL conference, Tucson, May 8-9, 1964. Champaign, Ill.: National Council of Teachers of English, 1965.

3 BRIÈRE, Eugène. "Testing the control of parts of speech in FL compositions," *LL* 14.1-10 (1964).

4 CLOSE, R. A. *English as a Foreign Language*. Cambridge: Harvard Univ. Press, 1963.

5 COCHRAN, Anne. *Modern Methods of Teaching English as a Foreign Language*, 2nd edition. Washington: Educational Services, 1954.

6 ESTACIO, C. I. C. "English syntax problems of Filipinos and the principles of linguistic relativity," *P9ICL* [**6.**15], 217-23.

7 FINOCCHIARO, Mary. *English as a Second Language: From Theory to Practice*. New York: Regents, 1964.

8 FRIES, Charles C. "American linguistics and the teaching of English," *LL* 6.1-22 (1955).

9 FRIES, Charles C. *Teaching and Learning English as a Foreign Language*. Ann Arbor: Univ. of Michigan Press, 1945.*

10 FRIES, Charles C. and Agnes C. *Foundations for English Teaching*. Tokyo: Kenkyusha, 1961.

11 GAUNTLETT, J. O. *Teaching English as a Foreign Language*. London: Macmillan, 1957.

12 GURREY, Percival. *Teaching English as a Foreign Language*. London, New York: Longmans, Green, 1955.

13 HILL, Leslie A. "Final clusters in English," *English Language Teaching* (London) 17.167-72 (1963).

14 HILL, Leslie A. "Noun-classes and the practical teacher." *LL* 9.23-32 (1959).

15 HILL, Leslie A. "The sequence of tenses with 'if'-clauses." *LL* 10.165-78 (1960).

16 HORNBY, A. S. "The situational approach in language teaching," *English Lang. Teaching* 4.98-103, 121-28, 150-56 (1950). Part III also in *TESL* [**71.**1].

17 ILSON, Robert. "The dicto-comp: a specialized technique for controlling speech and writing in language learning," *LL* 12.299-301 (1962).

18 LADO, Robert. *Language Testing: The Construction and Use of Foreign Language Tests*. London: Longmans, Green, 1961.*

19 MARCKWARDT, Albert H. "American English and British English," *ELEC Publications* 6.12-20 (1963). Tokyo: English Language Educational Council. Also in *TESL* [**71.**1].

20 MARCKWARDT, Albert H. "English as a second language and English as a foreign language," *PMLA* 78.25-8 (1963). Also in *TESL* [**71.**1].

21 PINCAS, Anita. "'Cultural translation' for foreign students of English language and literature," *LL* 13.15-25 (1963).

22 SHEN, Yao. *English Phonetics*. Ann Arbor, Mich.: Braun-Brumfield, 1962.

23 "Some likely areas of difficulty for Spanish students of English." *English: A New Language*. 8.2-17 (June 1961). Sydney: Australian Commonwealth Office of Education. Also in *TESL* [**71.**1].

1 STACK, Edward M. *The Language Laboratory and Modern Language Teaching.* New York: Oxford Univ. Press, 1960.

2 STEVICK, Earl W. *Helping People Learn English: A Manual for Teachers of English as a Second Language.* New York and Nashville: Abingdon Press, 1957.

3 STEVICK, Earl W. " 'Technemes' and the rhythm of class activity," *LL* 9:3.45-51 (1959).

Special Topics

Bilingualism

See also **1**.14, **64**.19-20, and *Language Instruction,* p. **67**.

4 ANASTASI, Anne, and Fernando A. CORDOVA. "Some effects of bilingualism upon the intelligence of Puerto Rican children in New York City," *Journal of Educational Psychology* 44.1-19 (1953).

5 BROSNAHAN, L. F. "Some aspects of the child's mastery of the sounds in a foster language," *SL* 14.85-94 (1960).

6 CHRISTOPHERSEN, Paul. *Bilingualism.* London: Methuen, 1948.

7 EMENEAU, Murray B. "Bilingualism and structural borrowing," *PAPS* 106.430-42 (1962).

8 FOWKES, Robert A. "Phonological aspects of Welsh-English bilingualism," *GL* 4.23-32 (1959).

9 HAUGEN, Einar. "Language contact," *P8ICL* [**6**.15], 771-85.

10 HOENIGSWALD, Henry M. "Bilingualism, presumable bilingualism, and diachrony," *AnL* 4.1-5 (1962).

11 JENSEN, J. Vernon. "Effects of childhood bilingualism," *Elementary English* 39.132-5, 358-66 (1962). [Bib.]

12 LEOPOLD, Werner F. *Speech Development of a Bilingual Child: A Linguist's Record.* Vol. 1, *Vocabulary Growth in the First Two Years* (1939); vol. 2, *Sound Learning in the First Two Years* (1947); vol. 3, *Grammar and General Problems in the First Two Years* (1949); vol. 4, *Diary from Age Two* (1949). Evanston, Ill.: Northwestern Univ. Press.

13 MACKEY, William F. "The description of bilingualism," *CJL* 7.51-85 (1962).

14 PIKE, Kenneth L. "Toward a theory of change and bilingualism," *SIL* 15.1-7 (1960).

15 READ, Allen Walker. "Bilingualism in the Middle Colonies 1725-1775," *AS* 12.93-9 (1937).

16 SINGER, Harry. "Bilingualism and elementary education," *MLJ* 40.444-59 (1956).

17 SWADESH, Morris. "Observations of pattern impact on the phonetics of bilinguals," *Language, Culture, and Personality* [**7**.1], 59-65.

18 VOGT, Hans. "Language contacts," *Word* 10.365-74 (1954).

Cant, Jargon, and Slang

See also **2.14**, **3.6**, **3.10**, **3.12**, **4.3-4**, **4.15**, **4.17**, and **27.9**.

1 ADAMS, Raymond F. *Cowboy Lingo*. Boston: Houghton Mifflin, 1936.

2 ANDREWS, Edmund. *A History of Scientific English: the Story of Its Evolution Based on a Study of Biomedical Terminology*. New York: Richard R. Smith, 1947.

3 ARNOLD, Jane W. "The language of delinquent boys." *AS* 22.120-23 (1947).

4 BERREY, Lester V., and Melvin VAN DEN BARK. *The American Thesaurus of Slang; A Complete Reference Book of Colloquial Speech*, 2nd edition. New York: Crowell, 1956.

5 BOONE, Lalia P. "Patterns of innovation in the language of the oil field." *AS* 24.31-37 (1949).

6 BURKE, W. J. *Literature of Slang*. New York: New York Public Library, 1939. [Bib.]

7 COLBY, Elbridge. *Army Talk*. Princeton: Princeton Univ. Press, 1942.

8 CUMMINGS, G. Clark. "The language of horse racing." *AS* 30.17-29 (1955).

9 DeCAMP, David, and Thomas Stell NEWMAN. "Smokejumping words." *AS* 33.180-84 (1958).

10 DEMPSEY, Don. "The language of traffic policemen." *AS* 37.266-73 (1962).

11 HARDER, Kelsie B. "The vocabulary of marble playing." *PADS* 23.3-33 (1955). [Addendum by Josiah H. Combs, 33-34.] See also **58.14**.

12 HEFLIN, Woodford A. "The airman's language." *Air Univ. Quarterly Rev.* 8.117-29 (1956).

13 HINTON, N. D. "The language of jazz musicians." *PADS* 30.38-48 (1958).

14 HOWARD, Donald. "United States Marine Corps slang." *AS* 31.188-94 (1956).

15 IRWIN, Godfrey. *American Tramp and Underworld Slang; Words and Phrases used by Hoboes, Tramps, Migratory Workers and Those on the Fringes of Society, with Their Uses and Origins, with a Number of Tramp Songs, Edited, with Essays on the Slang and the Songs. With a Terminal Essay on American Slang in its Relation to English Thieves' Slang, by Eric Partridge*. New York: Sears Publishing Co., 1931.

16 KRATZ, Henry. "What is college slang?" *AS* 39.188-95 (1964).

17 MAKOVSKIJ, M. M. "Interaction of areal slang variants and their correlation with standard language." *Linguistics* 7.42-54 (1964).

18 MAURER, David W. "Argot of the dice gambler." *Annals of the Am. Acad. of Pol. and Soc. Science* 269.114-33 (1950).

19 MAURER, David W. "The argot of the racetrack." *PADS* 16.70 (1951).

20 MAURER, David W. "Whiz mob; a correlation of the technical argot of pickpockets with their behavior pattern." *PADS* 24.1-199 (1955); "A word-finder for *Whiz Mob*," 31.14-30 (1959).

21 PARTRIDGE, Eric. *Slang Today and Yesterday; With a Short Historical Sketch; and Vocabularies of English, American, and Australian Slang*, 3rd edition, rev. and brought up to date. New York: Macmillan, 1950.

22 POSTON, Lawrence, III. "Some problems in the study of campus slang." *AS* 39.114-23 (1964).

23 RIPPY, Pauline. "Language trends in oil field jargon." *PADS* 15.72-80 (1951).

74 SPECIAL TOPICS

1 SELDEN, S. "Stage speech: kinesthetic influence," *Theater Arts* 29.420-1 (1945).

2 SHAFER, Robert. "The language of the West Coast culinary workers," *AS* 21.86-9 (1946).

3 SHAY, Frank. *A Sailor's Treasury; Being the Myths and Superstitions, Lore, Legends and Yarns, the Cries, Epithets, and Salty Speech of the American Sailorman in the Days of Oak and Canvas.* New York: Norton, 1951.

4 SHELLY, Loe. *Hepcats Jive Talk Dictionary.* Derby, Conn.: T. W. O. Charles Co., 1945.

5 SHERIDAN, P. H. D. "Timber Talk." *Tracks* (Chesapeake and Ohio Ry.) May 1950, 20-23.

6 SHULMAN, David. "Baseball's bright lexicon," *AS* 26.29-34 (1951).

7 SHULMAN, David. "Culinary Americanisms," *AS* 34.26-32 (1959).

8 SOBEL, Eli. "United States naval jargon and slang, 1942-45," *SFQ* 13.200-05 (1949).

9 TIDWELL, James N. "Political words and phrases: card-playing terms," *AS* 33.21-8 (1958).

Child Language

See also 1.19, 72.11-12.

10 ALBRIGHT, Robert W., and Joy Buck ALBRIGHT. "Application of descriptive linguistics to child language," *JSHR* 1.257-61 (1958).

11 ANASTASI, Anne, and Rita Y. D'ANGELO. "A comparison of Negro and white pre-school children in language development and Good-enough Draw-a-Man I.Q," *The Pedagogical Seminary and Journal of Genetic Psychology* 71:147-65 (1952).

12 APPLEGATE, Joseph R. "Phonological rules of a subdialect of English," *Word* 17.186-93 (1961).

13 BELLUGI, Ursula, and Roger BROWN, eds. *The Acquisition of Language: Report of the Fourth Conference Sponsored by the Committee on Intellective Processes Research of the Social Science Research Council.* Monographs of the Society for Research in Child Development 29. (1964).

14 BERKO, Jean. "The child's learning of English morphology," *Word* 14.150-77 (1958).

15 BRAINE, Martin D. S. "The ontogeny of English phrase structure: the first phase," *Lang* 39.1-13 (1963).

16 BROWN, Roger, and Jean BERKO. "Word association and the acquisition of grammar," *Child Development* 31.1-14 (1960).

17 BROWN, Roger, and Ursula BELLUGI. "Three processes in the child's acquisition of syntax," *HER* 34.133-51 (Spring, 1964).

18 FERGUSON, Charles A. "Baby-talk in six languages," *Ethnography* [5.15], 103-14.

19 IRWIN, O. C. "Phonetical description of speech development in childhood," *Manual of Phonetics* [6.7], 403-25.

20 LEWIS, M. M. *Infant Speech: A Study of the Beginnings of Language,* 2nd edition. New York: Humanities Press, 1951.*

21 LOBAN, Walter D. *The Language of Elementary School Children.* National Council of Teachers of English, Research report No. 1. Champaign, Ill.: National Council of Teachers of English, 1963.*

75

1 McCarthy, Dorothea. "Language development in children." *Manual of Child Psychology*, Leonard Carmichael, ed. 2nd ed., New York: Wiley, 1954. 492-630.

2 Menyuk, Paula. "A preliminary evaluation of grammatical capacity in children." *Journal of Verbal Learning and Verbal Behavior* 2.429-39 (1963).

3 Menyuk, Paula. "Syntactic rules used by children from preschool through first grade," *Child Development* 35.533-46 (1964).

4 Miller, Wick R. "Patterns of grammatical development in child language," *P9ICL* [**6**.15], 511-16.

5 Opie, Iona A., and Peter Opie. *The Lore and Language of Schoolchildren.* Oxford: Clarendon Press, 1960.

6 Piaget, Jean. *The Language and Thought of the Child.* New York: Meridian Books, 1958.*

7 Smillie, David. "Language development and lineality," *ETC: A Review of General Semantics* 17.203-8 (1960).

8 Strickland, Ruth G. *The Language of Elementary School Children: Its Relationship to the Language of Reading Textbooks and the Quality of Reading of Selected Children.* Bull. of the School of Education, Indiana Univ., Vol. 38, No. 4 (1962).*

9 Velten, Harry V. "The growth of phonemic and lexical patterns in infant language." *Language* 19.281-92 (1943).

10 Vygotsky, L. S. *Thought and Language.* Ed. and trans. by Eugenia Hanfmann and Gertrude Vakar. Cambridge: M. I. T. Press; New York: Wiley, 1962. [MIT 29]

11 Weir, Ruth Hirsch. *Language in the Crib.* 's-Gravenhage: Mouton, 1962.

Compounds

See also **16**.12, **36**.17, **85**.19, and **85**.21.

12 Ball, Alice M. *The Compounding and Hyphenation of English Words.* New York: H. W. Wilson, 1951.*

13 Bartlett, A. C. "Full-word compounds in modern English," *AS* 15.243-9 (1940).

14 Carr, Elizabeth. "Word-compounding in American speech," *SM* 26.1-20 (1959).

15 Hatcher, Anna Granville. "Bahuvrihi in Sears-Roebuck," *MLN* 59.515-26 (1944).

16 Hatcher, Anna Granville. "An introduction to the analysis of English noun compounds," *Word* 16.356-73 (1960).

17 Hatcher, Anna Granville. "Modern appositional compounds of inanimate reference," *AS* 27.3-15 (1952).

18 Hatcher, Anna Granville. *Modern English Word-formation and Neo-Latin; a Study of the Origins of English (French, Italian, German) Copulative Compounds.* Baltimore: Johns Hopkins Press, 1951. [Reviewed in *Lang* 27.597-601 (1951) by Fred Householder.]

19 Hunter, Edwin R. "Verb + adverb = noun," *AS* 22.115-19 (1947).

20 Marchand, Hans. *The Categories and Types of Present-Day English Word-Formation. A Synchronic-Diachronic Approach.* Wiesbaden: Harfassowitz, 1960; University, Ala.: Univ. of Alabama Press, 1966.

21 Sachs, Emmy. "On *steinalt, stock-still,* and similar formations," *JEGP* 62.581-96 (1963).

Etymology and Derivation

See also 3.19, 4.5, 4.10, 4.14, and WORD STUDIES ..., p. 66.

1 BARRS, James T. "The place of etymology in linguistics," *CE* 24.116-21 (1962).

2 HOUTZAGER, Maria E. *Unconscious Sound- and Sense-Assimilations.* Amsterdam: H. J. Paris, 1935.

3 LIVINGSTON, Charles H. *Skein-winding Reels: Studies in Word History and Etymology.* (UMPLL 29) Ann Arbor: Univ. of Michigan Press, 1957.

4 MALKIEL, Yakov. "Etymology and general linguistics," *Word* 18.198-219 (1962).

5 MALKIEL, Yakov. "A tentative typology of etymological studies," *IJAL* 22.1-17 (1957).

6 MALKIEL, Yakov. "The uniqueness and complexity of etymological solutions," *Lingua* 3.225-52 (1950).

7 MARCHAND, Hans. "On content as a criterion of derivational relationship with backderived words," *IF* 68.170-75 (1963).

8 MATHEWS, Mitford M. *Some Sources of Southernisms.* University, Ala.: Univ. of Alabama Press, 1948.

9 Ross, Alan S. C. *Etymology: With Especial Reference to English.* (The Language Library.) London: André Deutsch, 1958.

10 SKEAT, Walter William. *Principles of English Etymology.* 2 vols. Oxford: Clarendon Press, 1887-1891.*

11 SKEAT, Walter William. *The Science of Etymology.* Oxford: Clarendon Press, 1912.*

Graphemics, Writing, and the Alphabet

See also 83.2, 85.9-10, and 85.14.

12 ABERCROMBIE, David. "What is a 'letter'?" *Lingua* 11.54-63 (1949).

13 BERRY, J. "The making of alphabets," *P8ICL* [6.15], 752-64.

14 BREKLE, H. E. "Statistical correlation between typographical data and spelling-variants in 16th and 17th century English books: a contribution to diachronic English morphographemics," *Linguistics* 9.13-28 (1964).

15 CHAO, Yuen Ren. "Graphic and phonetic aspects of linguistic and mathematical symbols," *Structure of Language* [6.5], 69-82.

16 CLODD, Edward. *The Story of the Alphabet.* New York: Appleton-Century-Crofts, 1938.

17 DIRINGER, David. *The Alphabet: A Key to the History of Mankind,* 2nd edition. New York: Philosophical Library, 1953.*

18 DIRINGER, David: *Writing: Its Origin and Early History.* New York: Praeger, 1962.

19 DRIVER, Godfrey R. *Semitic Writing: From Pictograph to Alphabet,* revised edition. London: Oxford Univ. Press, 1954.

20 EDGERTON, W. F. "Ideograms in English writing," *Lang* 17.148-50 (1941).

21 FISHER, John H. "The ancestry of the English alphabet," *Archaeol.* 4.232-42 (1951).

22 FRANCIS, W. Nelson. "Graphemic analysis of late Middle English manuscripts," *Speculum* 37.32-47 (1962).

1 GELB, Ignace J. *A Study of Writing*, 2nd edition. Chicago: Univ. of Chicago Press, 1963 [Phoen P109].*

2 GIBSON, Eleanor J., Harry OSSER, and Anne D. PICK. "A study of the development of grapheme-phoneme correspondences," *Journal of Verbal Learning and Verbal Behavior* 2.142-6 (1963).

3 HAMP, Eric P. "Graphemics and paragraphemics," *SIL* 14.1-5 (1959).

4 IRWIN, Keith Gordon. *The Romance of Writing: From Egyptian Hieroglyphics to Modern Letters, Numbers, and Signs*. New York: Viking Press, 1956.

5 JOHNSON, Elmer D. *Communication. A Concise Introduction to the History of the Alphabet, Writing, Printing, Books and Libraries*. New Brunswick, N. J.: Scarecrow Press, 1955.

6 McINTOSH, Angus. " 'Graphology' and meaning," *ArL* 13.107-20 (1961).

7 MERCER, Samuel A. B. *Origin of Writing and Our Alphabet*. London: Luzac and Co. Ltd., 1959.

8 MOORHOUSE, A. C. *Writing and the Alphabet*. London: Cobbett Press, 1946.

9 PULGRAM, Ernst. "Phoneme and grapheme: a parallel," *Word* 7.15-20 (1951).

10 STOCKWELL, Robert P., and Westbrook BARRITT. "Scribal practice: some assumptions," *Lang* 37.75-82 (1961).

Idiom

See also **3.7**.

11 BLISS, A. J. "A Modern English idiom," *Anglia* 73.320-21 (1956).

12 COLLINS, Henry Vere. *A Third Book of English Idioms, with Explanations*. London: Longmans, Green, 1960.

13 FARIS, Paul. "As far as halfbacks, we're all right," *AS* 37.236-8 (1962).

14 HOCKETT, Charles F. "Idiom formation," *For Roman Jakobson* [5.16], 222-9.

15 ORR, J. *Old French and Modern English Idiom*. Oxford: Blackwell, 1962.

16 RAUN, Alo. "Concerning idiomatic features," *Lingua* 11.331-32 (1959).

17 ROBERTS, Murat H. "The science of idiom: a method of inquiry into the cognitive design of language," *PMLA* 59.291-306 (1944).

18 SMITH, Logan Pearsall. *Words and Idioms: Studies in the English Language*. Boston: Houghton, Mifflin, 1925.

19 WHITFORD, Harold C., and Robert James DIXSON. *Handbook of American Idioms and Idiomatic Usage*. New York: Regents, 1952.

20 WOOD, Frederick T. *English Verbal Idioms*. New York: St. Martin's Press, 1964.

International Language

GENERAL

21 CLARK, Emery. "John Wilkins' universal language," *Isis* 38.174-85 (1947). [On his *Essay towards a Real Character and a Philosophical Language*.]

22 CONNOR, George Allen, *et al. Esperanto. The World Interlanguage*, rev. ed. New York: Thomas Yoseloff, 1959.

1 COPI, Irving M. "Artificial languages," *Language, Thought, and Culture* [**6.2**], 96-120.

2 GODE, Alexander, and Hugh E. BLAIR. *Interlingua: A Grammar of the International Language*. New York: Storm Publishers, 1951.

3 JACOB, Henry. *A Planned Auxiliary Language*. New York: Dover, 1957.

4 JESPERSEN, Otto. *An International Language*. London: Allen & Unwin, 1928.

5 McQUOWN, Norman A. "A planned auxiliary language," *Lang* 26.175-85 (1950). Also in *Language in Culture and Society* [**6.3**], 555-63. Review of Jacob [**78.3**].

6 SHARPE, Lawrence A. "Artificial language projects," *SAB* 27.1-6 (1961).

7 WHITMORE, Charles E. "The problem of a universal language," *The Scientific Monthly* 71.337-42 (1950).

8 WILLIAMS, John E. *The Basis of Pikto*. Pikto International Union: Bushey, Herts., 1959.

BASIC ENGLISH

9 BONGERS, H. "Basic English." *ES* 27.161-74 (1946).

10 COLLINSON, W. E. "Basic English as an international language," *TPS*, 1945, 121-36.

11 HABER, Tom Burns. "The present status of Basic English in the United States," *QJS* 34.483-9 (1948).

12 JOHNSEN, Julia E., compiler. *Basic English*. (The Reference Shelf, Vol. 17, No. 1.) New York: H. W. Wilson, 1944.

13 OGDEN, Charles K. *Basic English versus the Artificial Languages*. London: Kegan Paul, 1935.

14 OGDEN, Charles K. *The System of Basic English*. New York: Harcourt, Brace and World, 1934.

15 WYNBURNE, S. B. "Basic English for the analysis of 'meaning'," *ETC.* 15.21-9 (1957).

PIDGIN

16 BAKER, Sidney John. "The literature of pidgin English," *AS* 19.271-5 (1944).

17 HALL, Robert A., Jr. *Hands off Pidgin English!* New York: Albert Daub, 1956.

18 HALL, Robert A., Jr. "The life cycle of pidgin languages," *Lingua* 11.151-6 (1962).

19 HALL, Robert A., Jr. *Melanesian Pidgin English: Grammar, Texts, Vocabulary*. Baltimore: Linguistic Society of America. 1943.

20 HALL, Robert A., Jr. "Pidgin languages," *Scientific American* 200.124-34 (Feb. 1959).*

21 LEECHMAN, Douglas, and Robert A. HALL, Jr. "American Indian Pidgin English: Attestations and grammatical peculiarities," *AS* 30.162-71 (1955).

22 LePAGE, Robert B. "General outlines of Creole English dialects in the British Caribbean," *Orbis* 6.373-91; 7.54-64 (1957, 1958). See also **62.2**.

Kinesics and Paralinguistics

See also 1.15.

1   BIRDWHISTELL, Ray L. "Background to kinesics," *ETC.* 13.10-18 (1955).

2   BIRDWHISTELL, Ray L. *Introduction to Kinesics.* Washington: Foreign Service Institute, 1952.*

3   CRITCHLEY, MacDonald. *The Language of Gesture.* London: Edwin Arnold; New York: Longmans, Green, 1939. [Rev. by Robert West, *QJS* 26.456 (1940).]

4   HALL, Edward T. *The Silent Language.* New York: Doubleday, 1959. [Prem. R204].*

5   KROEBER, A. L. "Sign language inquiry," *IJAL* 24.1-19 (1958).

6   RUESCH, Jurgen, and Weldon KEES. *Nonverbal Communication; Notes on Visual Perception of Human Relations.* Berkeley: Univ. of California Press, 1956.

7   SEBEOK, Thomas A., Alfred S. HAYES, and Mary Catherine BATESON. *Approaches to Semiotics.* Transactions of the Indiana Univ. Conference on Paralinguistics and Kinesics. 's-Gravenhage: Mouton, 1964.

8   TRAGER, George L. "Paralanguage: a first approximation," *SIL* 13.1-12 (1958).*

9   VOEGELIN, Carl F. "Sign language analysis, on one level or two?" *IJAL* 24.71-7 (1958).

Lexicography

10   AARSLEFF, Hans. "The early history of the *Oxford English Dictionary*," BNYPL 66.417-39 (1962).

11   ALDEN, Donald H. "The first pronouncing dictionary," *QJS* 22.12-18 (1936).

12   ANTAL, László. "A new type of dictionary," *Linguistics* 1.75-84 (1963).

13   BARNHART, Clarence L. "Problems in editing commercial monolingual dictionaries," *IJAL* 28.161-81 (1962). Also in *Problems in Lexicography* [**80**.3] and *RAEL* [**5**.1], 457-75.

14   BURKETT, Eva. "The American Samuel Johnson and his dictionaries," *PQ* 19:3.295-305 (1940).

15   CHAPMAN, R. W. *Lexicography.* London: Oxford Univ. Press, 1948.

16   CRAIGIE, Sir William A. "The value of the period dictionaries," *TPS 1936* 53-62 (1937).

17   DYKEMA, Karl W. "Cultural lag and reviewers of Webster III," *AAUP Bull.* 49.364-9 (1963).

18   EMSLEY, Bert. "The first 'phonetic' dictionary," *QJS* 28.202-6 (1942).

19   GOVE, Philip B. "Lexicography and the teacher of English," *CE* 25.344-52, 357 (1964).

20   GOVE, Philip B. " 'Noun often attributive' and 'adjective'," *AS* 39.163-75 (1964).

21   HIORTH, Finngeir. "Arrangement of meanings in lexicography," *Lingua* 4.413-24 (1955).

1 HIORTH, Finngeir. "On the foundations of lexicography," *SL* 11.8-27 (1957).

2 HIORTH, Finngeir. "On the relationship between field research and lexicography," *SL* 10.57-66 (1956).

3 HOUSEHOLDER, Fred W., and Sol SAPORTA, eds. *Problems in Lexicography.* (PRCAFL no. 21) Bloomington: Indiana Univ., 1962.

4 HULBERT, J. R. *Dictionaries, British and American.* New York: Philosophical Library, 1955.

5 KEAST, W. R. "Johnson's *Plan of a Dictionary:* a textual crux," *PQ* 33.341-7 (1954).

6 KENYON, John S. "Syllabic consonants in dictionaries," *AS* 31.243-51 (1956).

7 KNOTT, Thomas A. "How the dictionary determines what pronunciation to use," *QJS* 21.1-10 (1935).

8 MARCKWARDT, Albert H. "Dictionaries and the English language," *EJ* 52.336-45 (1963).

9 MATHEWS, Mitford M. "Problems encountered in the preparation of a dictionary of American words and meanings," *EIE,* 1947 (New York: Columbia Univ. Press, 1948), 76-96.

10 MATHEWS, Mitford M. *A Survey of English Dictionaries.* London: Oxford Univ. Press, Humphrey Milford, 1933.*

11 NIDA, Eugene A. "Analysis of meaning and dictionary-making," *IJAL* 24.279-92 (1958).

12 OSSELTON, N. E. *Branded Words in English Dictionaries Before Johnson.* (Groningen Studies in English, 7). Groningen: J. B. Wolters, 1958.

13 READ, Allen Walker. "The labeling of national and regional variation in popular dictionaries," *IJAL* 28.217-27 (1962).

14 READ, Allen Walker. "Projected English dictionaries," *JEGP* 36:2.188-205; 3.347-66 (1937).

15 ROSIER, James L. "Lexical strata in Florio's *New World of Words,*" *ES* 44.415-23 (1963).

16 ROSIER, James L. "The sources and methods of Minsheu's 'Guide into the Tongues'," *PQ* 40.68-76 (1961).

17 SEBEOK, Thomas A. "Materials for a typology of dictionaries," *Lingua* 11.363-74 (1962).

18 SHELDON, Esther K. "Pronouncing systems in eighteenth-century dictionaries," *Lang* 22.27-41 (1946).

19 SLEDD, James H., and Gwin J. KOLB. *Dr. Johnson's Dictionary: Essays in the Biography of a Book.* Chicago: Univ. of Chicago Press, 1955.

20 SLEDD, James H., and Wilma R. EBBITT. *Dictionaries and* That *Dictionary.* Chicago: Scott, Foresman, 1962.

21 SMALLEY, Vera E. *The Sources of* A Dictionarie of the French and English Tongue *by Randle Cotgrave (London 1611), A Study in Renaissance Lexicography.* Baltimore: Johns Hopkins Stud. in Romance Lit. and Lang., extra vol. 25.

22 STARNES, DeWitt T. *Renaissance Dictionaries: English-Latin and Latin-English.* Austin: Univ. of Texas Press, 1954.*

23 STARNES, DeWitt, and Gertrude E. NOYES. *The English Dictionary from Cawdrey to Johnson, 1604-1755.* Chapel Hill: Univ. of North Carolina Press, 1946.*

Lexicostatistics (Glottochronology)

1 BERGSLAND, K., and Hans VOGT. "On the validity of glottochronology," *CAn* 5.115-29 (1962).

2 CARROLL, John B., and Isidore DYEN. "High-speed computation of lexicostatistical indices," *Lang* 38.274-8 (1962).

3 CHRÉTIEN, C. Douglas. "The mathematical models of glottochronology," *Lang* 38.11-37 (1962).*

4 DYEN, Isidore. "On the validity of comparative lexicostatistics," With disc. by Horace G. Lunt, *P9ICL* [6.15], 238-52.

5 FAIRBANKS, Gordon H. "A note on glottochronology," *IJAL* 21.116-20 (1955).

6 GLEASON, H. A., Jr. "Genetic relationship among languages," *Structure of Language* [6.5], 179-89.

7 GUDSCHINSKY, Sarah C. "The ABC's of lexicostatistics (glottochronology)," *Word* 12.175-210 (1956).*

8 GUDSCHINSKY, Sarah C. "Three disturbing questions concerning lexicostatistics," *IJAL* 22.212-13 (1956).

9 HOCKETT, Charles F. "Linguistic time-perspective and its anthropological uses," *IJAL* 19.146-52 (1953). [Comment by Morris Swadesh, 152-3.]

10 HOIJER, Harry. "Lexicostatistics: a critique," *Lang* 32.49-60 (1956).

11 HYMES, Dell. "Lexicostatistics so far," With bib. *Current Anthropology* 1.3-44 (1960).

12 KROEBER, A. L. "Romance history and glottochronology," *Lang* 34.454-57 (1958).

13 KROEBER, A. L., and C. Douglas CHRÉTIEN. "Quantitative classification of Indo-European languages," *Lang* 13.83-103 (1937).

14 LEES, Robert B. "The basis of glottochronology," *Lang* 29.113-27 (1953).

15 REA, John A. "Concerning the validity of lexicostatistics," *IJAL* 24.145-50 (1958).

16 SWADESH, Morris. "Lexicostatistic dating of prehistoric ethnic contacts," *PAPS* 96.452-63 (1952).*

17 SWADESH, Morris. "Towards greater accuracy in lexicostatistic dating," *IJAL* 21.121-37 (1955).

Linguistic Geography (Dialect Geography)

See also **15**.1, **33**.5, and DIALECTS, p. **58**.

18 ABERCROMBIE, David. "The recording of dialect material," *Orbis* 3.231-35 (1954).

19 ATWOOD, E. Bagby. "The methods of American dialectology," *ZMF* 30:1.1-29 (1963).

20 BONFANTE, Giuliano, and Thomas A. SEBEOK. "Linguistics and the age and area hypothesis," *AA* 46.382-86 (1944).

21 BOTTIGLIONI, Gino. "Linguistic geography: achievements, methods, and orientation," *Word* 10.375-87 (1954).

22 CATFORD, John C. "The linguistic survey of Scotland," *Orbis* 6.105-21 (1957).

82 SPECIAL TOPICS

1   GROOTAERS, Willem A. "Origin and nature of the subjective boundaries of dialects," *Orbis* 8.355-84 (1959).

2   HEGEDUS, L. "Experimental phonetics in the service of the linguistic atlas," *ALASH* 5.185-217 (1955).

3   HILL, Trevor. "Phonemic and prosodic analysis in linguistic geography," *Orbis* 12.449-55 (1963).

4   IVIĆ, Pavle. "On the structure of dialectal differentiation," *Word* 18.33-53 (1962).

5   IVIĆ, Pavle. "Structure and typology of dialectal differentiation," *P9ICL* [6.15], 115-19.

6   KURATH, Hans. *Handbook of the Linguistic Geography of New England.* Providence, R.I.: Brown Univ., 1939. See also **59**.12.

7   KURATH, Hans. "Interrelation between regional and social dialects," *P9ICL* [6.15], 135-43.

8   McINTOSH, Angus. *An Introductory Survey of Scottish Dialects.* Edinburgh: Thomas Nelson, 1952.

9   McINTOSH, Angus. "Patterns and ranges," *Lang* 37.325-37.

10 MOULTON, William G. "Dialect geography and the concept of phonological space," *Word* 18.23-32 (1962).

11 ORTON, Harold, and Eugen DIETH. *Survey of English Dialects: Introduction.* Leeds: E. J. Arnold (for the Univ. of Leeds), 1962.

12 ORTON, Harold, and Wilfred J. HALLIDAY, eds. *Survey of English Dialects.* Vol. 1, *Basic Material: Six Northern Counties and Man.* Leeds: E. J. Arnold (for the Univ. of Leeds), Part 1, 1962; Pts. 2 and 3, 1963.

13 REED, David W., and John L. SPICER. "Correlation methods of comparing idiolects in a transition area," *Lang* 28.348-59 (1952).

14 SEREBRENNIKOV, B. A. "The history of languages and areal linguistics," *P8ICL* [6.15], 119-21.

15 STANKIEWICZ, Edward. "On discreteness and continuity in structural dialectology," *Word* 13.44-59 (1957).

16 STOCKWELL, Robert P. "Structural dialectology: a proposal," *AS* 34.258-68 (1959).

17 ULSTER FOLK MUSEUM. *Ulster Dialects.* An Introductory Symposium. Holywood, Co. Down, Northern Ireland: Ulster Folk Museum, 1965.

18 WAGNER, H. *Linguistic Atlas and Survey of Irish Dialects,* Vol. 1. Dublin: Institute for Advanced Studies, 1959.

19 WEINREICH, Uriel. "Is a structural dialectology possible?" *Word* 10.388-400 (1954).

Linguistics and Reading

20 BLOOMFIELD, Leonard. "Linguistics and Reading," *LL* 5:3&4.94-107 (1952-3). [Repr. from *Elementary Engl. Rev.* 19.125-30, 183-86 (1942).] *

21 BLOOMFIELD, Leonard, and Clarence L. BARNHART. *Let's Read: A Linguistic Approach.* Detroit, Mich.: Wayne State Univ. Press, 1961.

22 BRUNER, Jerome S., and Donald O'DOWD. "A note on the informativeness of parts of words," *L&S* 1.98-102 (1958).

23 FRIES, Charles C. *Linguistics and Reading.* New York: Holt, Rinehart and Winston, 1962.*

1 HAGBOLT, P. "Physiological and psychological aspects of reading," *Curme Studies* [5.17], 84-91.

2 HALL, Robert A., Jr. *Sound and Spelling in English.* Philadelphia: Chilton Co., 1961.*

3 HALL, Robert A., Jr. "Thorstein Veblen and linguistic theory," *AS* 35.124-30 (1960).

4 KING, Harold V. "Linguistic aspects of the reading program," *LL* 9.19-23 (1959).

5 LEFEVRE, Carl A. *Linguistics and the Teaching of Reading.* New York: McGraw-Hill, 1964.

6 ROBINSON, Francis P. "The effect of language style on reading performance," *Jrnl. of Educ. Psych.* 38.149-56 (1947).

7 ROBINSON, H. Alan, ed. *Reading and the Language Arts. (Supplementary Educational Monographs,* No. 93). Chicago: Univ. of Chicago Press, 1964.

8 SOFFIETTI, James P. "Why children fail to read; a linguistic analysis," *HER* 25:2.63-84 (1955).

Onomastics

See also 2.9-10, 2.15, 3.1, 3.3, 3.5, 3.18, 4.7-8, 4.18, and 27.8.

9 ADAMIC, Louis. *What's Your Name?* New York: Harper and Row, 1942.

10 ALEXANDER, W. H. "The purposive study of names," *Names* 2.169-72 (1954).

11 ASIMOV, Isaac. *Words on the Map.* Boston: Houghton Mifflin, 1962.

12 AUROUSSEAU, M. *The Rendering of Geographical Names.* New York: Holt, Rinehart and Winston, 1957.

13 BOWMAN, William Dodgson. *The Story of Surnames.* New York: Knopf, 1931.

14 BRENDER, Myron. "Some hypotheses about the psychodynamic significance of infant name selection," *Names* 11.1-9 (1963).

15 BURRILL, Meredith F. "Toponymic generics," *Names* 4.129-37, 226-40 (1956).

16 CAMERON, Kenneth. *English Place-names.* London: B. T. Batsford, 1961.

17 CASSIDY, Frederic G. *The Place-names of Dane County, Wisconsin.* (Foreword by Robert L. Ramsay.) *PADS* no. 7, 1947.*

18 CLIFFORD, Colonel E. H. M. "Recording native place names," *The Geographical Journal* 109.99-102 (1947).

19 CRAY, Ed. "Ethnic and place names as derisive adjectives," *WF* 21.27-34 (1962).

20 EKWALL, Eilert. *Street-names of the City of London.* Oxford: Clarendon Press, 1954.

21 EWEN, C. L'Estrange. *A History of British Surnames.* London: Routledge, 1931.

22 FELDMAN, Harold. "The problem of personal names as a universal element in culture," *AI* 16.237-50 (1959).

23 FUCILLA, Joseph G. *Our Italian Surnames.* Evanston, Ill.: Chandler's, 1949.

24 GANNETT, Henry. *American Names: A Guide to the Origin of Place Names in the United States.* Washington, D.C.: Public Affairs Press, 1947.

1 GARDINER, Sir Alan H. *The Theory of Proper Names: A Controversial Essay.* London: Oxford Univ. Press, 1940.

2 GELB, Ignace J. "Ethnic reconstruction and onomastic evidence." *Names* 10.45-52 (1962).

3 GUDDE, Erwin G. *California Place Names: The Origin and Etymology of Current Geographical Names,* rev. and enl. edition. Berkeley: Univ. of California Press, 1960.

4 HOLMER, Nils M. *Indian Place Names in North America.* Cambridge: Harvard Univ. Press, 1948.

5 MAURER, Warren R. "Another view of literary onomastics," *Names* 11.106-14 (1963).

6 McATEE, W. L. "Nationality names for American birds," *AS* 32.180-85 (1957).

7 McMILLAN, James B. "Observations on American place-name grammar," *AS* 24.241-8 (1949); "A further note." 27.196-8 (1952).

8 McMULLEN, E. Wallace. *English Topographic Names in Florida 1563–1874.* Gainesville: Univ. of Florida Press, 1953.

9 MENCKEN, Henry L. "Names for Americans," *AS* 22.241-56 (1947).

10 PEARSALL, W. H. "Place-names as clues in the pursuit of ecological history," *NB* 49.72-89 (1961).

11 PLANK, Robert. "Names and roles of characters in science fiction," *Names* 9.151-9 (1961).

12 PULGRAM, Ernst. "Theory of names," *BN* 5.149-96 (1954).

13 PYLES, Thomas. "Onomastic individualism in Oklahoma," *AS* 22.257-64 (1947).

14 RAMSAY, Robert L. *Our Storehouse of Missouri Place Names.* Columbia, Mo.: Univ. of Missouri, 1952.*

15 REANEY, P. H. A. *The Origin of English Place-Names.* New York: Hillary House, 1961.

16 SHANKLE, G. E. *American Nicknames, their Origin and Significance,* 2nd ed. New York: H. W. Wilson, 1955.

17 SMITH, A. H. *English Place-Name Elements.* Cambridge: Cambridge Univ. Press, 1956.

18 SMITH, Elsdon C. "Concerning American surnames and their relation to eminence," *Names* 10:38-44 (1962).

19 SMITH, Elsdon C. *The Story of Our Names.* New York: Harper, 1950.

20 SØRENSEN, Holger Steen. *The Meaning of Proper Names, with a Definiens Formula for Proper Names in Modern English.* Copenhagen: G. E. C. Gad, 1963.

21 STEWART, George R. *Names on the Land; A Historical Account of Place-naming in the United States,* rev. ed. Boston: Houghton Mifflin, 1958.*

22 UTLEY, Francis Lee. "The linguistic component of onomastics," *Names* 11.145-76 (1963).*

23 WOOLF, Henry B. *The Old Germanic Principles of Name-Giving.* Baltimore: Johns Hopkins Press, 1939.

24 WRAIGHT, A. J. "Field work in the U.S.C. and G.S.," *Names* 2:153-63 (1954). [Naming by the U.S. Coast and Geodetic Survey.]

25 ZACHRISSON, R. E. "The meaning of English place-names in the light of the terminal theory," *SN* 6.25-89 (1934).

1   ZELINSKY, Wilbur. "Some problems in the distribution of generic terms in the place-names of the Northeastern United States," *Annals of the Assoc. of American Geographers* (1955), 319-49.

2   ZINK, Sidney. "The meaning of proper names," *Mind* 72.481-99 (1963).

Orthography and Spelling Reform

See also **83**.2 and *Graphemics,* p. **76**.

3   CRAIGIE, Sir William A. *English Spelling, Its Rules and Reasons.* New York: Appleton-Century-Crofts, 1927.*

4   CRAIGIE, Sir William A. *Problems of Spelling Reform.* (*Society for Pure English,* Tract No. 63 (1940), 47-75.

5   CRAIGIE, Sir William A. *Some Anomalies of Spelling.* (*Society for Pure English,* Tract No. 59). Oxford: Clarendon Press, 1942.

6   DAVIS, Norman. "Scribal variation in late fifteenth-century English," *Mélanges Fernand Mossé* [6.12], 95-103.

7   EMERY, Donald W. "Variant spellings," *CCC* (NCTE) 11.55-8 (1960).

8   EUSTACE, S. Sinclair. "English spelling-reform: a new and holistic approach," *P8ICL* 1958 [6.15], pp. 153-5.

9   HIGGINBOTTOM, Eleanor M. "A study of the representation of English vowel phonemes in the orthography," *L&S* 5.67-117 (1962).

10 LESTER, Mark. "Graphemic-phonemic correspondences as the basis for teaching spelling," *Elementary English* 41.748-52 (1964).

11 OSSELTON, N. E. "Formal and informal spelling in the 18th century: *errour, honor,* and related words," *ES* 44.267-75 (1963).

12 POLLOCK, Thomas C. "Spelling report," *CE* 16.102-9 (1954). [A survey.]

13 TAUBER, Abraham. "Spelling breaks thru," *CUF* 7.50-52 (1964).

14 TRAGER, Edith Crowell. "The systematics of English spelling," *CCC* (NCTE) 8.26-32 (1957).

15 VALLINS, G. H. *Spelling.* With chapter on American spelling by John W. Clark. London: Deutsch, 1954.

16 WIJK, Axel. *Regularized English; An Investigation into the English Spelling Reform Problem with a New, Detailed Plan for a Possible Solution.* (Stockholm Studies in English, No. 7) Stockholm: Almqvist and Wiksell, 1959.

17 ZACHRISSON, R. E. "Four hundred years of English spelling reform," *SN* 4.1-69 (1931).

Punctuation

See also **75**.12.

18 BROSNAHAN, L. F. "The apostrophe in the genitive singular in the 17th century," *ES* 42.313-19 (1961).

19 HALL, Robert A., Jr. "To hyphenate or not to hyphenate," *EJ* 53.662-65 (1964). [Phonological basis for punctuating compounds.]

20 HONAN, Park. "Eighteenth and nineteenth century English punctuation theory," *ES* 41.92-102 (1960).

21 JONES, Daniel. "The hyphen as a phonetic sign," *Zeitschrift für Phonetik* 9.99-107 (1956).

22 McCUTCHEON, R. J. "The serial comma before 'and' and 'or'," *AS* 15.250-54 (1940).

1 MICHAELSON, L. W. "Atrophy of the apostrophe," *WSt* 36.5-6 (1961).

2 ONG, Walter J. "Historical backgrounds of Elizabethan and Jacobean punctuation theory," *PMLA* 59.349-60 (1944).

3 SØRENSEN, Holger S. "An analysis of linguistic signs occurring in *suppositio materialis,* or the meaning of quotation marks and their phonetic quivalents," *Lingua* 10.174-89 (1961).

4 SUMMEY, George, Jr. *American Punctuation.* New York: Ronald Press, 1949.*

Stylistics; Linguistics and Prosody

See also 6.20 and 83.6.

5 ABERCROMBIE, David. "A phonetician's view of verse structure," *Linguistics* 6.5-13 (1964).

6 AXELROD, J. "Cummings and phonetics," *Poetry* 55.88-94 (1944).

7 BLANKENSHIP, Jane. "A linguistic analysis of oral and written style," *QJS* 48.419-22 (1962).

8 BOGGS, W. Arthur. "A linguistic definition of poetry," *BNYPL* 66.97-100 (1962).

9 BOLINGER, Dwight L. "Rime, assonance, and morpheme analysis," *Word* 6.117-36 (1950).

10 CANNON, Garland. "Linguistics and literature," *CE* 21.255-60 (1960).

11 CHATMAN, Seymour. "Linguistics, poetics, and interpretation: the phonemic dimension," *QJS* 43.248-56 (1957). [Reply by John C. McLaughlin, *QJS* 44.175-8 (1958).]

12 CHATMAN, Seymour. "Robert Frost's *Mowing:* an inquiry into prosodic structure," *KR* 18.421-38 (Summer, 1956).

13 CHATMAN, Seymour. *A Theory of Meter.* 's-Gravenhage: Mouton, 1965.*

14 DEGROOT, A. Willem. "The description of a poem," *P9ICL* [6.15], 294-300.

15 DEVOTO, G. *Linguistics and Literary Criticism.* New York: S. F. Vanni, 1963.

16 DUNDES, Allen. "From etic to emic units in the structural study of folktales," *Journal of American Folklore* 75.95-105 (1962).

17 EPSTEIN, Edmund L., and Terence HAWKES. *Linguistics and English Prosody.* (SILOP no. 7). Buffalo: Univ. of Buffalo, 1959.

18 FRANCIS, W. Nelson. "Syntax and literary interpretation," *Monograph Series on Language and Linguistics* No. 13. Washintgon: Georgetown University Press, 1962. Also in *RAEL* [5.1], 514-22.

19 GARVIN, Paul L., ed. and transl. *A Prague School Reader on Esthetics, Literary Structure and Style.* Washington: Georgetown Univ. Press, 1964.

20 HALLIDAY, M. A. K. "The linguistic study of literary texts," *P9ICL* [6.15], 302-7.

21 HILL, Archibald A. "An analysis of *The Windhover:* an experiment in structural method," *PMLA* 70.968-78 (1955).

22 HILL, Archibald A. "Pippa's song: two attempts at structural criticism," Univ. of Texas *Studies in English,* 35.51-56 (1956).

23 HILL, Archibald A. "Principles governing semantic parallels," *TSLL* 1.356-65 (1959). Also in *RAEL* [5.1], 506-14.

1   JAKOBSON, Roman. "Closing statement: linguistics and poetics." *Style in Language* [6.20], 350-77.

2   LEVIN, Samuel R. *Linguistic Structures in Poetry*. 's-Gravenhage: Mouton, 1962.

3   LEVIN, Samuel R. "Poetry and grammaticalness," *P9ICL* [6.15], 308-14.

4   LEVIN, Samuel R. "Suprasegmentals and the performance of poetry," *QJS* 48.366-72 (1962).

5   LOTZ, John. "Metric typology," *Style in Language* [6.20], 135-48.

6   OHMANN, Richard. "Generative grammars and the concept of linguistic style," *Word* 20.423-39 (1964).

7   PACE, George. "The two domains: meter and rhythm," *PMLA* 74.413-19 (1961).

8   PECKHAM, Morse, and Seymour CHATMAN. *Word, Meaning, Poem*. New York: Crowell, 1961.

9   PIKE, Kenneth L. "Language—where science and poetry meet," *CE* 26.283-86, 291-92 (1965).

10 RIFFATERRE, Michael. "Criteria for a style analysis," *Word* 15.154-74 (1959).

11 RUS, Louis C. "Structural ambiguity: a note on meaning and the linguistic analysis of literature, with illustrations from E. E. Cummings," *LL* 6.62-7 (1955).

12 SAPORTA, Sol. "The application of linguistics to the study of poetic language," *Style in Language* [6.20], 82-93.

13 SPENCER, John, M. GREGORY, and N. ENKVIST. *Linguistics and Style*. London: Oxford Univ. Press, 1965. [Reviewed by David Crystal, *JL* 1.173-9 (1965).]

14 STANKIEWICZ, Edward. "Linguistics and the study of poetic language," *Style in Language* [6.20], 69-81.

15 SUTHERLAND, Ronald. "Structural linguistics and English prosody," *CE* 20.12-17 (1958). Also in *RAEL* [5.1], 492-99.

16 THORNE, J. P. "Stylistics and generative grammars," *JL* 1.49-59 (1965). [A separate grammar for each text.]

17 ULLMANN, Stephen. *Language and Style: Collected Papers*. Oxford: Blackwell, 1964.

18 UTLEY, Francis Lee. "Structural linguists and the literary critic," *JAAC* 18.319-28 (March 1960).

19 WELLS, Rulon S. "Nominal and verbal style," *Style in Language* [6.20], 213-220.

20 WHITEHALL, Harold. "From linguistics to criticism," *KR* 13.710-14 (1951).

21 WHITEHALL, Harold, Seymour CHATMAN, Arnold STEIN, John Crowe RANSOM. "English verse and what it sounds like," *KR* 18.411-77 (1956).

22 WIMSATT, W. K., Jr., and Monroe C. BEARDSLEY. "The concept of meter: an exercise in abstraction," *PMLA* 74.585-98 (1959).

Taboo and Euphemism

See also 4.3 and 4.17.

23 ELEASBERG, W. "Remarks on the psychopathology of pornography," *Jrnl. Criminal Psychopathology* 3.715 (1942).

1   FRYER, Peter. *Mrs. Grundy; Studies in English Prudery.* London: Dennis Dobson, 1963.

2   GRAVES, Robert. *The Future of Swearing.* London: Routledge, Kegan Paul, 1936.

3   HAAS, Mary R. "Interlingual word taboos," *AA* 53.338-44 (1951).

4   HUNTER, Edwin R., and Bernice E. GAINES. "Verbal taboo in a college community," *AS* 13.97-107 (1938).

5   MacCULLOCK, J. A. "Euphemism," *Encyclopedia of Religion and Ethics,* James Hastings, ed. New York: C. Scribner's Sons, 1912, vol. 5, 585-8.

6   MONTAGU, M. F. Ashley. "On the physiology and psychology of swearing," *Psychiatry* 5.189 (1942).

7   POUND, Louise. "American euphemisms for dying, death, and burial: An anthology," *AS* 11.195-202 (1936).

8   PYLES, Thomas. "Innocuous linguistic indecorum: a semantic byway," *MLN* 44.1-8 (1949).

9   READ, Allen Walker. "An obscenity symbol," *AS* 9.264-78 (1934).

10   SAGARIN, Edward. *The Anatomy of Dirty Words.* New York: Lyle Stuart, 1962. [With introd. by Allen Walker Read.]

11   STEADMAN, J. M., Jr. "A study of verbal taboos," *AS* 10.93-103 (1935).

12   STONE, Leo. "On the principal obscene word of the English language," *International Journal of Psycho-analysis* 35.30 (1954). [Bib.]

13   TASSIE, J. S. "The use of sacrilege in the speech of French Canada," *AS* 36.34-41 (1961).

Translation

See also 2.1, 5.7, 7.3 and *Computational and Mathematical . . .* , p. 9.

14   ANDREYEV, N. D. "Linguistic aspects of translation," *P9ICL* [6.15], 625-34.

15   BROWER, Reuben A., ed. *On Translation.* (*HSCL* No. 23) Cambridge: Harvard Univ. Press, 1959.*

16   CASAGRANDE, Joseph B. "The ends of translation," *IJAL* 20.335-40 (1954).

17   CHAO, Yuen Ren. "Translation without machine," *P9ICL* [6.15], 504-10.

18   FIRTH, John R. "Linguistic analysis and translation," *For Roman Jakobson* [5.16], 133-9.

19   FRENZ, Horst. "The art of translation," *Comparative Literature: Method and Perspective,* Stallknecht, Newton P., and Horst Frenz, eds. Carbondale, Ill.: Univ. Press, 1961.

20   HOCKETT, Charles F. "Translation via immediate constituents," *IJAL* 20.313-15 (1954).

21   KNOX, Ronald Arbuthnott. *On English Translation.* (The Romanes Lecture for 1957). Oxford: Clarendon Press, 1957.

22   LONGACRE, Robert E. "Items in context: their bearing on translation theory," *Lang* 34.482-91 (1958).

23   MAYMI, P. "Grammatical principles and techniques in language translation," *Hispania* 42.233-38 (1959).

24   NIDA, Eugene A. "Principles of translation as exemplified by Bible translating," *On Translation* [**88**.15], 11-31.

25   NIDA, Eugene A. *Toward a Science of Translating.* Leiden: Brill, 1964.

1   Rabin, C. "The linguistics of translation," *Aspects of Translation* [5.7], 123-45.

2   Salzmann, Zdenek. "Cultures, languages, and translations," *AnL* 2:2.43-7 (1960).

3   Savory, Theodore. *The Art of Translation.* London: Cape, 1957.

4   Swadesh, Morris. "On the unit of translation," *AnL* 2:2.39-42 (1960).

ADDENDA 91

Bibliographies
See page 1.

DINGWALL, William Orr. *Transformational Generative Grammar: A Bibliography*. Washington, D.C.: Center for Applied Linguistics, 1965.

OHANNESIAN, Sirarpi, and Ruth E. WEINBERG. *Teaching English as a Second Language in Adult Education: An Annotated Bibliography*. Washington: Center for Applied Linguistics, 1966.

SABLESKI, Julia A. "A selective annotated bibliography on child language," *LingR* 7.4-6 (1965).

SHAUGHNESSY, Amy E., ed. *Dissertations in Linguistics*. Washington, D.C.: Center for Applied Linguistics, 1965.

WALTERS, T. W., S.J. *The Georgetown Bibliography of Studies Contributing to the Psycholinguistics of Language Learning*. Washington, D.C.: Georgetown Univ. Press, 1965.

Dictionaries and Glossaries
See page 2.

PEI, Mario. *A Glossary of Linguistic Terminology*. New York: Columbia Univ. Press, 1966. [Anchor A497].

Festschriften and Miscellaneous Collections
See page 5.

VACHEK, Josef, compiler. *A Prague School Reader in Linguistics*. Bloomington: Indiana Univ. Press, 1964. [Reviewed by Yakov Malkiel, *AA* 68. 585-7 (1966).]

Linguistics

General Linguistics
See page 7.

ABERCROMBIE, David. *Studies in Phonetics and Linguistics*. London: Oxford Univ. Press, 1965.

DINEEN, Francis P., S.J. *An Introduction to General Linguistics*. New York: Holt, Rinehart and Winston, 1967.

GARVIN, Paul L. *On Linguistic Methods: Selected Papers*. 's-Gravenhage: Mouton, 1964.

LONGACRE, Robert E. *Grammar discovery procedures: A field manual.* (Janua Linguarum, series minor, No. 33) 's-Gravenhage: Mouton, 1964. [Reviewed by Wallace L. Chafe, *Lang* 41.640-7 (1965).]

MARTINET, André. *Elements of General Linguistics,* transl. by Elisabeth Palmer. Chicago: Univ. of Chicago Press, 1964. [Reviewed by Robert A. Hall, Jr. in *Lang* 41.493-504 (1965).]

STREVENS, Peter D. *Papers in Language and Language Teaching.* London: Oxford Univ. Press, 1965.

Communication Theory and Information Theory
See page 9.

ABRAMSON, Norman. *Information Theory and Coding.* New York: McGraw-Hill, 1964.

WEAVER, Carl H. and Garry L. "Information theory and the measurement of meaning," *SM* 32.435-47 (1965).

Computational and Mathematical Linguistics; Machine Translation and Information Retrieval

KAY, Martin, and Theodore ZIEHE. *Natural Language in Computer Form.* Santa Monica, Calif.: Rand Corp., 1965.

SEDELOW, Sally Y., and Walter A., Jr. *A Preface to Computational Stylistics.* (SDC Document, SP-1534) Santa Monica, Calif.: Systems Development Corporation, 1964.

Linguistic Theory
See page 11.

CHOMSKY, Noam. "The current scene in linguistics: present directions," *CE* 27.587-95 (1966).

CHOMSKY, Noam, and Morris HALLE. "Some controversial questions in phonological theory," *JL* 1.97-138 (1965).

CHRÉTIEN, C. Douglas. "General linguistics and the probability model," *Lang* 42.518-30 (1966).

GLEASON, H. A., Jr. "The organization of language: a stratificational view," *Monograph Series on Languages and Linguistics,* No. 17. Washington: Georgetown Univ. Press, 1964.

HJELMSLEV, L., and H. J. ULDALL. *An Outline of Glossematics.* Copenhagen: Travaux du Cercle Linguistique de Copenhague, 1957.

LAMB, Sydney M. "Epilogomena to a theory of language," *RPh* 19.531-73 (1966).

LAMB, Sydney M. "On alternation, transformation, realization, and stratification," *Monograph Series on Languages and Linguistics,* No. 17, Washington: Georgetown Univ. Press, 1964.

LAMB, Sydney M. *Outline of Stratificational Grammar.* With an appendix by Leonard E. Newell, "Stratificational analysis of an English text." Washington: Georgetown Univ. Press, 1966.

LAMB, Sydney M. "Prolegomena to a theory of phonology," *Lang* 42.536-73 (1966).

LAMB, Sydney M. "The sememic approach to structural semantics," *AA* 66. 57-78 (1964).

LEES, Robert B. "On the testability of linguistic predicates," *Linguistics* 12.37-48 (1965).

LEVIN, Samuel R. "Langue and parole in American linguistics," *FL* 1.83-94 (1965).

LONGACRE, Robert E. "Some fundamental insights of tagmemics," *Lang* 41.65-76 (1965).

SIERTSEMA, Berta. *A Study of Glossematics: A Critical Survey of Its Fundamental Concepts.* 's-Gravenhage: Martinus Nijhoff, 1955.

SWADESH, Morris. "Language universals and research efficiency in descriptive linguistics," *CJL* 10.147-55 (1965).

WILSON, Robert D. "A criticism of distinctive features," *JL* 2.195-206 (1966).

ZIMMER, Karl E. *Affixal Negation in English and Other Languages: An Investigation of Restricted Productivity* (Supplement to *Word* 20.2, Monograph No. 5). New York, 1964. [Reviewed by Hans Marchang, *Lang* 42. 134-42 (1966).]

Generative Grammar and Transformation Grammar
See page 15.

CHOMSKY, Noam. "On certain formal properties of grammars," *Readings in Mathematical Psychology* 15.125-55 (1965).

CHOMSKY, Noam. "Three models for the description of language," *Readings in Mathematical Psychology* 15.105-24 (1965).

CLOSS, Elizabeth. "Diachronic syntax and generative grammar," *Lang* 41. 402-15 (1965).

COOK, Walter, S.J. *On Tagmemes and Transforms.* Washington, D.C.: Georgetown Univ. Press, 1964.

HARRIS, Zellig S. "Transformational Theory," *Lang* 41.363-401 (1965).

KOUTSOUDAS, Andreas. *Writing Transformational Grammars: An Introduction.* New York: McGraw-Hill, 1966.

THOMAS, Owen. *Transformational Grammar and the Teacher of English.* New York: Holt, Rinehart and Winston, 1965. [Reviewed by Paul Schachter, *HER* 35.513-16 (1965).]

WINTER, Werner. "Transforms without kernels?" *Lang* 41.484-9 (1965).

The Study of Linguistics and of Grammar, and the History of Linguistic Thought
See page 17.

IVIĆ, Milka. *Trends in Linguistics.* 's-Gravenhage: Mouton, 1965.

JAKOBSON, Roman. "Boas' view of grammatical meaning," *AA* 41.139-45 (1959).

TEETER, Karl V. "Descriptive linguistics in America: Triviality vs. irrelevance," *Word* 20.197-206 (1964).

VACHEK, Josef. *The Linguistic School of Prague.* Bloomington: Indiana Univ. Press, 1964.

VORLAT, Emma. *Progress in English Grammar, 1585-1735:* A Study of the Development of English Grammar and of the Interdependence among the Early English Grammarians. 4 vols. Louvain: Catholic Univ. of Louvain, 1963.

Biographies of Linguists
See page **19**.

SEBEOK, Thomas A., ed. *Portraits of Linguists.* A Biographical Source Book for the History of Western Linguistics, 1746-1963. Bloomington: Indiana Univ. Press, 1966.

Phonetics

GENERAL
See page **22**.

FRIES, Charles C. "On the intonation of 'Yes-No' questions in English," *In Honor of Daniel Jones* [5.11], 242-54.

GREENBERG, Joseph H. "Some generalizations concerning initial and final consonant sequences," *Linguistics* 18.5-34 (1965).

GREENBERG, Joseph H. "Synchronic and diachronic universals in phonology," *Lang* 42.508-17 (1966).

HULTZÉN, Lee S. "Grammatical intonation," *In Honour of Daniel Jones* [5.11], 85-95.

JAKOBSON, Roman, C. GUNNAR, M. FANT, and Morris HALLE. *Preliminaries to Speech Analysis: Distinctive Features and Their Correlates.* Cambridge, Mass.: M.I.T. Press, 1963.

LEHISTE, Ilse. *Acoustical Characteristics of Selected English Consonants.* Bloomington, Ind.: Indiana Univ. Press, 1964. [Reviewed by Peter Ladefoged, *Lang* 41.332-8 (1965).]

WINTER, Werner. *Evidence for Laryngeals.* 's-Gravenhage: Mouton, 1965.

HISTORICAL (PHONOLOGY)
See page **26**.

HOCKETT, Charles F. "Sound change," *Lang* 41.185-204 (1965).

Psycholinguistics; the Psychology of Language
See page **26**.

BERNSTEIN, Basil. "Linguistic codes, hesitation phenomena, and intelligence," *L&S* 5.31-46 (1962).

BOOMER, Daniel S. "Hesitation and grammatical encoding," *L&S* 8.148-58 (1965).

DECECCO, John P., ed. *The Psychology of Language, Thought, and Instruction.* New York: Holt, Rinehart and Winston, 1967.

GREENBERG, Joseph H., and James J. JENKINS. "Studies in the psychological correlates of the sound system of American English," *Word* 20.157-77 (1964).

HOCKETT, Charles F. "Ethnolinguistic implications of studies in linguistics and psychiatry," *Monograph Series on Languages and Linguistics*, No. 11. 175-93. Washington, D.C.: Georgetown Univ. Press, 1960.

LENNEBERG, Eric H., ed. *New Directions in the Study of Language.* Cambridge: M.I.T. Press, 1964. [MIT-56].

SLAMA-CAZACU, Tatiana. "Essays on psycholinguistic methodology and some of its applications," *Linguistics* 24.51-72 (1966).

Semantics: Language and Philosophy

GENERAL

See page **28**.

LUGTON, Robert C. "Wittgenstein's theories of language," *Occasional Papers* 1.5-27 (1965), A Publication of the American Language Institute, New York Univ.

LYONS, J. *Structural Semantics: An Analysis of Part of the Vocabulary of Plato.* Oxford: PPS XX, 1963. [Reviewed by Jeffrey Ellis, *Linguistics* 24. 85-115 (1966).]

MORRIS, Charles W. *Signification and Significance.* Cambridge, Mass.: M.I.T. Press, 1964.

LINGUISTIC (SEMASIOLOGY)

See page **30**.

GEORGE, F. H. *Semantics.* London: English Univ. Press, 1964.

SØRENSEN, Holger Steen. *Word Classes in English with Special Reference to Proper Names, with an Introductory Theory of Grammar, Meaning, and Reference.* Copenhagen: Gad, 1958.

Sociolinguistics; Language and Culture
See page **32**.

BOCK, Philip K. "Social structure and language structure," *SJA* 20.393-403 (1964).

CAPELL, A. *Studies in Socio-Linguistics.* 's-Gravenhage: Mouton, 1966.

LABOV, William. *The Social Stratification of English in New York City.* Washington: Center for Applied Linguistics, 1966.

McDAVID, Raven I., Jr. "Dialect differences and social differences in an urban society," in Robert F. Hogan, ed., *The English Language in the School Program*, Champaign, Ill.; National Council of Teachers of English, 1966.

ROBINSON, W. P. "Cloze procedure as a technique for the investigation of social class differences in language usage," *L&S* 8.42-55 (1965).

Structural Comparison, Comparative Linguistics, and Typology
See page **34**.

DINGWALL, William Orr. "Morpheme sequence classes: a taxonomic approach to contrastive analysis," *IRAL* 4.39-61 (1966).

KRUPA, Viktor. "On quantification of typology," *Linguistics* 12.31-6 (1965).

LEVENSON, E. A. "A classification of language differences," *IRAL* 4.199-206 (1966).

STOCKWELL, Robert P., and J. D. BOWEN. *The Sounds of English and Spanish: A Systematic Analysis of the Contrasts between the Sound Systems.* Chicago and London: Univ. of Chicago Press, 1965.

STOCKWELL, Robert P., J. D. BOWEN, and J. W. MARTIN. *The Grammatical Structures of English and Spanish: An Analysis of Structural Differences Between the Two Languages.* Chicago and London: Univ. of Chicago Press, 1965.

English Language and English Linguistics

Backgrounds of English: Indo-European (especially Germanic)
See page 37.

ANTONSEN, Elmer H. "On defining stages in prehistoric Germanic," *Lang* 41.19-36 (1965).

CARDONA, George. "On Pānini's morphophonemic principles," *Lang* 41. 225-37 (1965).

JONES, Oscar F. "The case for a long *u*-phoneme in Wulfilian Gothic," *Orbis* 14.393-405 (1965).

PULLEYBLANK, E. G. "The Indo-European vowel system and the qualitative ablaut," *Word* 21.86-101 (1965).

History of the English Language

GENERAL

See page 39.

BARBER, Charles. *Linguistic Change in Present-Day English*. Edinburgh & London: Oliver & Boyd, 1964; University, Ala.: Univ. of Alabama Press, 1965.

NIST, John. *A Structural History of English*. New York: St. Martin's Press, 1966.

MIDDLE ENGLISH

See page 45.

BERNDT, Rolf. "The linguistic situation in England from the Norman Conquest to the loss of Normandy (1066-1204)," *PP* 8.145-63 (1965).

McLAUGHLIN, John C. *A Graphemic-Phonemic Study of a Middle English Manuscript*. 's-Gravenhage: Mouton, 1963). [Reviewed by Elliott V. K. Dobbie, *Lang* 41.151-4 (1965).]

Present-day English Grammar

GENERAL

See page 49.

ALLEN, Robert L. *The Verb System of Present-Day American English*. 's-Gravenhage: Mouton, 1966.

BOLINGER, Dwight L. *Forms of English: Accent, Morpheme, Order*. Cambridge, Mass.: Harvard Univ. Press, 1965.

MORPHEMICS

See page 50.

LEBRUN, Yvan, and Jacques DEVOOGHT. "Quantitative relations between 'can' and 'may'," *ZAA* 13. 161-6 (1965).

Phonemics

See page 51.

Pierce, Joe E. "The supra-segmental phonemes of English," *Linguistics* 21.54-70 (1966).

Sledd, James H. "Breaking, umlaut, and the Southern drawl," *Lang* 42.18-41 (1966).

Smith, Henry Lee, Jr. "Superfixes and syntactic markers," *Monograph Series on Languages and Linguistics,* No. 9. Washington, D.C.: Georgetown Univ. Press, 1957.

Trager, George L. "The intonation system of American English," *In Honour of Daniel Jones* [5.11], 266-70.

Phonetics

See page 52.

Pierce, Joe E. "The morphemes of English: morphemic theory," *Linguistics* 23.90-7 (1966).

Syntax

See page 54.

Bowman, Elizabeth. *The Minor and Fragmentary Sentences of a Corpus of Spoken English.* Publication 42 of Indiana University Research Center in Anthropology, Folklore, and Linguistics; = Pt. 2 of vol. 32, no. 3, of *IJAL.* Bloomington, Ind.: Indiana Univ. Press, 1966.

Gleitman, Lila R. "Coordinating conjunctions in English," *Lang* 41.260-93 (1965).

Pilch, Herbert. "Comparative constructions in English," *Lang* 41.37-58 (1965).

American English

General

See page 57.

Francis, W. Nelson. "A standard corpus of edited present-day American English," *CE* 26.267-73 (1965).

Kurath, Hans. "British sources of selected features of American pronunciation: problems and methods," *In Honour of Daniel Jones* [5.11], 146-55.

Dialects

See page 58.

Kurath, Hans. "Regionalism in American English," in *The English Language in the School Program,* Robert F. Hogan, ed. Champaign, Ill.: National Council of Teachers of English, 1966. Pp. 161-175.

Commonwealth English: Australia, Canada, Jamaica, South Africa

See page 61.

Jones, J. Allen. "English in the Commonwealth: 9. The West Indies," *English Lang. Teaching* 20.145-52 (1966).

RYAN, J. S. "Isolation and generation within a conservative framework—A unique dialectal situation for English," *Orbis* 15.35-50 (1966). [Australian English.]

Usage

GENERAL
See page 62.

GODFREY, Judith A. "The survey of English usage," *English Lang. Teaching* 19.98-103 (1965).

WARBURG, Jeremy. "Discriminations in judging linguistic expressions," *E&S* 18.103-18 (1965).

HISTORY OF ATTITUDES TOWARD USAGE
See page 63.

HOLMBERG, Börje. "Noah Webster and American pronunciation," *ES* 46. 118-29 (1965).

HOLMBERG, Börje. *On the Concept of Standard English and the History of Modern English Pronunciation.* Lunds Universitets Årsskrift, vol. 56, no. 3. Lund: Gleerup, 1964.

Vocabulary

GROWTH AND MEASUREMENT
See page 64.

JONES, Lyle V., and Joseph M. WEPMAN. *A Spoken Word Count.* Chicago: Language Research Associates, 1966.

LOANWORDS IN ENGLISH FROM OTHER LANGUAGES
See page 65.

THOMSON, R. L. "The Celtic element in the English vocabulary," *ULR* 8.212-22 (1963).

Language Instruction

General Studies

POLITZER, Robert L. *Foreign Language Learning,* prelim. ed. Englewood Cliffs, N.J.: Prentice-Hall, 1965.

POLITZER, Robert L. "The impact of linguistics on language teaching: past, present and future," *MLJ* 48.146-51 (1964).

SPOLSKY, Bernard. "A psycholinguistic critique of programmed foreign language instruction," *IRAL* 4.119-29 (1966).

SPOLSKY, Bernard. "Computer-based instruction and the criteria for pedagogical grammars," *LL* 15.137-45 (1965).

VAN TESLAAR, A. P. "Learning new sound systems: problems and prospects," *IRAL* 3.79-93 (1965).

English to English Speakers (Grammar, Composition, etc.)
See page **69**.

BATEMAN, Donald, and Frank ZIDONIS. *The Effect of a Study of Transformational Grammar on the Writing of Ninth and Tenth Graders.* Research Report No. 6. Champaign, Ill.: National Council of Teachers of English, 1966.

BECKER, A. L. "A tagmemic approach to paragraph analysis," *CCC (NCTE)* 16.237-42 (1965).

HUNT, Kellogg W. *Grammatical Structures Written at Three Grade Levels* (NCTE Research Report No. 3). Champaign, Ill.: NCTE, 1965.

Language, Linguistics and School Programs. Proceedings of the 1963 Spring Institutes of the NCTE. Reviewed by F. Gomes de Matos, *Linguistics* 25.78-80 (1966).

MARCKWARDT, Albert H. *Linguistics and the Teaching of English.* Bloomington, Ind.: Indiana Univ. Press, 1966.

HOGAN, Robert F., ed. *The English Language in the School Program.* Champaign, Ill.: National Council of Teachers of English, 1966.

McDAVID, Raven I., Jr. "Dialect study and English education," in *New Trends in English Education,* David Stryker, ed. Champaign, Ill.: NCTE, 1966, 43-52.

PIKE, Kenneth L. "Beyond the sentence," *CCC* (NCTE) 15.129-35 (1964).

ROSENBAUM, Peter S. "On the role of linguistics in the teaching of English," *HER* 35.332-48 (1965).

SHUY, Roger W., ed. *Social Dialects and Language Learning.* Champaign, Ill.: National Council of Teachers of English, 1965.

SLEDD, James H. "On not teaching English usage," *EJ* 54.698-703 (1965).

STREVENS, Peter. "Phonetics, applied linguistics, and other components of language teaching," *In Honour of Daniel Jones* [5.11], 120-8.

YOUNG, Richard E., and Alton L. BECKER. "Toward a modern theory of rhetoric: a tagmemic contribution," *HER* 35.450-68 (1965).

English to Speakers of Other Languages (English as a Second Language)
See page **70**.

BELASCO, Simon. "Nucleation and the audio-lingual approach," *MLR* 49.482-91 (1965).

KREIDLER, Carol J., ed. *On Teaching English to Speakers of Other Languages.* Series II: Papers read at the TESOL conference, San Diego, Calif., March 12-13, 1965. Champaign, Ill.: NCTE, 1966.

Special Topics

Bilingualism
See page **72**.

ANDERSON, Theodore. "A new focus on the bilingual child," *MLJ* 49.156-60 (1965).

Bilingualism and the Bilingual Child—A Symposium. MLJ 49 (Special Issue, 1965).

FISHMAN, Joshua A. "Bilingualism, intelligence and language learning," *MLJ* 49.227-37 (1965).

FISHMAN, Joshua A. *Language Loyalty in the United States.* 's-Gravenhage: Mouton, 1966.

FISHMAN, Joshua A. "Status and prospects of bilingualism in the United States," *MLJ* 49.143-55 (1965).

GARDNER, A. Bruce. "Teaching the bilingual child: research, development and policy," *MLJ* 49.165-75 (1965).

HAUGEN, Einar. "Dialect, Language, Nation," *AA* 68.922-35 (1966).

HAUGEN, Einar. *Language Conflict and Language Planning: The Case of Modern Norwegian.* Cambridge, Mass.: Harvard Univ. Press, 1965.

Child Language
See page 74.

LOBAN, Walter D. *The Language of Elementary School Children.* Research Report No. 1. Champaign, Ill.: National Council of Teachers of English, 1963.

International Language

PIDGIN

See page 78.

HALL, Robert A., Jr. *Pidgin and Creole Languages.* Ithaca, N.Y.: Cornell Univ. Press, 1966. [Reviewed by R. Bosteels in *Orbis* 15.319-25 (1966).]

WHINNOM, Keith. "The origin of the European-based Creoles and Pidgins (I)," *Orbis* 14.509-27 (1965).

Kinesics and Paralinguistics
See page 79.

AUSTIN, William M. "Some social aspects of paralanguage," *CJL* 11.31-9 (1965).

CRYSTAL, David, and Randolph QUIRK. *Systems of Prosodic and Paralinguistic Features in English.* (Janua Linguarum, series minor, no. 39) 's-Gravenhage: Mouton, 1964.

HAYES, Alfred S. "Paralinguistics and kinesics: pedagogical perspectives," *Approaches to Semiotics* [79.7], 145-72.

Lexicography
See page 79.

HELLER, Louis G. "Lexicographic etymology: practice versus theory," *AS* 40.113-19 (1965).

OSSELTON, N. E. "Early bi-lingual dictionaries as evidence for the status of words in English," *ES* 45 (supplement). 14-20 (1964).

Lexicostatistics (Glottochronology)
See page 81.

DYEN, Isidore. "Lexicostatistics in comparative linguistics," *Lingua* 13.230-39 (1965).

Onomastics
See page **83**.

FUNKE, Otto. "On the function of naming: a problem of general semasiology," *ES* 18.57-62 (1936).

Stylistics; Linguistics and Prosody
See page **86**.

CHATMAN, Seymour, and Samuel R. LEVIN, eds. *Essays on the Language of Literature.* New York: Houghton Mifflin, 1967.

LEVIN, Samuel R. "Deviation—statistical and determinate—in poetic language," *Lingua* 12.276-90 (1964). [Reply to Robert J. Scholes, "Some objections to Levin's 'Deviation'," *Lingua* 13.189-92 (1965).]

MOWATT, D. G., and P. F. DEMBOWSKI. "Literary study and linguistics," *CJL* 11.40-62 (1965).

Translation
See page **88**.

CATFORD, J. C. *A Linguistic Theory of Translation.* London: Oxford Univ. Press, 1965.

NOTES

INDEX

B

Bull, William E., **12**.18
Burchfield, R. W., **45**.10
Burke, Kenneth, **12**.19, **28**.16
Burke, W. J., **73**.6
Burkett, Eva, **79**.14
Burrill, Meredith F., **83**.15
Bursill-Hall, G. L., **1**.6, **17**.15-16
Byrne, Sister St. Geraldine, **47**.21

Caffee, Nathaniel M., **5**.6, **51**.21
Callaway, Morgan, Jr., **41**.4, **42**.21, **50**.12
Calver, Edward, **50**.13
Cameron, Kenneth, **83**.16
Campbell, Alistair, **42**.22
Cannon, Charles D., **62**.20
Cannon, Garland, **7**.7, **86**.10
Capell, A., **95**.7
Cardona, George, **96**.2
Carey, G. V., **60**.17
Carlton, Charles, **43**.1
Carnap, Rudolf, **28**.17-18-19
Carnochan, J., **19**.16
Carr, Charles T., **38**.1, **65**.20
Carr, Elizabeth, **75**.14
Carranco, Lynwood, **58**.12
Carroll, John B., **15**.13, **15**.19, **17**.17, **21**.2, **27**.3, **32**.24, **67**.23, **81**.2
Carter, C. W., Jr., **53**.9
Casagrande, Joseph B., **88**.16
Cassidy, Frederic G., **40**.17, **50**.14, **58**.13-14, **62**.2, **83**.17
Cassirer, Ernst, **28**.20-21
Castle, William E., **24**.10
Catford, John C., **81**.22, **101**.5
Chao, Yuen Ren, **21**.3, **76**.15, **88**.17
Chapman, R. W., **79**.15
Charleston, Britta M., **30**.20, **50**.15, **55**.6, **64**.21
Charnley, M. Bertens, **12**.20, **55**.7
Chase, J. P., **9**.20
Chatman, Seymour, **12**.21, **43**.2, **55**.8-9, **86**.11-12-13, **87**.8, **87**.21, **101**.2
Cherry, E. Colin, **9**.7-8
Chomsky, Noam, **12**.22-23, **15**.20-21-22, **16**.1-2, **27**.4, **28**.22, **51**.22, **92**.8-9, **93**.8-9
Chrétien, C. Douglas, **81**.3, **81**.13, **92**.10

Christensen, Francis, **62**.21
Christophersen, Paul, **55**.10, **72**.6
Cioffari, Vincenzo, **68**.1
Clark, Emery, **77**.21
Clark, G. N., **65**.21
Clark, John Williams, **40**.6, **85**.15
Clark, Joseph D., **58**.15
Cleator, P. E., **7**.8
Cleave, John P., **9**.21
Clifford, Colonel E. H. M., **83**.18
Clodd, Edward, **76**.16
Close, R. A., **71**.4
Closs, Elizabeth, **93**.10
Cochran, Anne, **71**.5
Cofer, Charles N., **27**.20
Cohen, A., **24**.11, **51**.23
Cohen, Marcel, **33**.1
Colby, Elbridge, **73**.7
Collinge, N. E., **12**.24, **26**.10, **41**.5
Collins, Henry Vere, **77**.12
Collinson, W. E., **35**.5, **36**.18, **50**.16, **78**.10
Collitz, Hermann, **38**.2
Collitz, Klara H., **30**.21
Congleton, J. E., **63**.24
Conklin, Harold C., **33**.2
Conner, J. E., **45**.11
Connor, George Allen, **77**.22
Contreras, Heles, **13**.1
Cook, Walter, **93**.11
Cooper, Franklin S., **25**.16
Copi, Irving M., **78**.1
Copley, J., **30**.22
Corder, S. Pit, **68**.2
Cordova, Fernando A., **72**.4
Couillard, Louis E., **33**.3
Cowan, H. K. J., **35**.6
Coxe, M. S., **25**.21
Craigie, Sir William A., **2**.18, **79**.16, **85**.3-4-5
Crawford, John, **26**.9
Cray, Ed, **83**.19
Critchley, MacDonald, **79**.3
Crossland, R. A., **10**.1
Crystal, David, **100**.12
Culbert, Sidney S., **30**.23
Cummings, G. Clark, **73**.8
Curme, George O., **35**.7, **50**.17, **55**.11, **69**.19

111